THE POWER OF SENSITIVITY

Finding Your Strength as a Highly Sensitive Person

JUDY DYER

THE POWER OF SENSITIVITY:
Finding Your Strength as a Highly Sensitive Person
by Judy Dyer

© Copyright 2022 by Judy Dyer

All Rights Reserved.

No part of this publication may be reproduced, distributed, or transmitted in any form or by any means, including photocopying, recording, or other electronic or mechanical methods, without the prior written permission of the publisher, except in the case of brief quotations embodied in reviews and certain other noncommercial uses permitted by copyright law.

Disclaimer: This book is designed to provide accurate and authoritative information in regard to the subject matter covered. By its sale, neither the publisher nor the author is engaged in rendering psychological or other professional services. If expert assistance or counseling is needed, the services of a competent professional should be sought.

ISBN: 979-8846745452

ALSO BY JUDY DYER

Empath: A Complete Guide for Developing Your Gift and Finding Your Sense of Self

The Empowered Empath: A Simple Guide on Setting Boundaries, Controlling Your Emotions, and Making Life Easier

Empath Children: How to Help a Highly Sensitive Child Thrive and Stop Feeling Overwhelmed

The Power of Emotions: How to Manage Your Feelings and Overcome Negativity

Empath and The Highly Sensitive: 2 Books in 1

Empaths and Narcissists: 2 Books in 1

Narcissist: A Complete Guide for Dealing with Narcissism and Creating the Life You Want

Anger Management: How to Take Control of Your Emotions and Find Joy in Life

Borderline Personality Disorder: A Complete BPD Guide for Managing Your Emotions and Improving Your Relationships

CONTENTS

Introduction 7

Your Free Gift—Heyoka Empath 15

Chapter 1: The Highly Sensitive Person—Traits
and Characteristics 21

Chapter 2: How to Set up Your Home Environment 30

Chapter 3: The Importance of Diet and Exercise 40

Chapter 4: How Negative Energy Affects Highly
Sensitive People 60

Chapter 5: How to Beat Emotional Overload 86

Chapter 6: Letting People Into Your Highly Sensitive
World 95

Chapter 7: Dealing With Depression as a Highly
Sensitive Person 127

Chapter 8: Dealing With Anxiety as a Highly Sensitive
Person 133

Chapter 9: In The Pursuit of Wholeness 148

Chapter 10: Self-care Tips For Highly Sensitive People 161

Conclusion 170

INTRODUCTION

According to Dr. Elaine Aron, approximately 20-30 percent of the population are highly sensitive. Isn't that fantastic? You are not alone in this battle; research suggests it's actually pretty common. The problem is that no one talks about high sensitivity, psychologists have limited awareness of it because it's not a mental illness (which is good news), and you won't find it listed in the *Diagnostic and Statistical Manual of Mental Disorders*. Although the personality trait comes with many challenges, such as emotional overwhelm, overthinking, and anxiety, it is a very powerful quality to have if you know how to manage it.

When you're a highly sensitive person (HSP), life can feel like it's spinning out of control. You often feel as if you're on a never-ending roller coaster of emotions. Things that everyone else can just brush off send you into a frenzy. Minor irritations turn your stomach, make your palms sweat, and zap your energy. No one understands you, and you're made to feel like a freak because you don't function like the average person. Anxiety is your best friend, and you've learned to accept that there's not much you can do about it. But I've got some good news for you: You can live a fulfilling and vibrant life as a highly sensitive person.

Let me tell you how I know this.

Just over four years ago, I was a struggling highly sensitive person. I hated leaving the house, I couldn't stand being in a group setting, and I'd become lonely and bitter. Not because I wanted to be, but because that was the only way I knew how to cope. I developed a terrible habit of binge eating to get me through the day, I was nervous and anxious most of the time, and most people I came into contact with thought I was pretty strange. Deep down, I knew something wasn't quite right, but I didn't know where to start. But destiny has a strange way of locating you. After my father died, I got so depressed that I needed therapy. My therapist's name was Jasmine. I assumed she was going to treat me for depression, but it just so happened that she was a highly sensitive person, and she picked up on my high sensitivity immediately. For the first time in my life, I looked forward to leaving the house. I sat on the edge of my chair and soaked up Jasmine's every word because I knew I had found the antidote to the hell I had been living in for so many years.

My therapist and I both experienced the world on a distinctive frequency. We were intuitive, deep thinkers, and naturally empathetic. She was also prone to depression and anxiety. The only difference between us was that she understood her gift in a way that I didn't, and she had strategically organized her life to ensure she experienced the full benefits of being highly sensitive. Now Jasmine was passing the baton on to me. I was inspired to learn that she too once suffered from what I call "the curse of high sensitivity." Her story gave me hope that I would one day experience all the advantages of being a highly sensitive person—and today, I can say with confidence that I love my unique personality trait.

Highly sensitive brothers and sisters, I want to remind you that the wings you've been given are for flying. You are destined for greater heights, and another dimension awaits you. Within these pages you will find the tools you need to overcome anxiety, depression, emotional overload and everything else that burdens you as you navigate this alternate reality of ours. I will provide you with specific strategies to help you live life to the fullest as a highly sensitive person.

Today doesn't have to be like yesterday—your gift can be a blessing if you want it to be. Turn the page... It's time to soar into new realms of possibilities!

JOIN OUR SUPPORT GROUP

In order to maximize the value you receive from this book, I highly encourage you to join our tight-knit community on Facebook. There you will be able to connect and share with other like-minded Empaths and HSPs to continue your growth.

Taking this journey alone is not recommended, and this can be an excellent support network for you.

It would be great to connect with you there,

Judy Dyer

To Join, Visit:
www.facebook.com/groups/EmpathGift/

DOWNLOAD THE AUDIO VERSION OF THIS BOOK FOR FREE

If you love listening to audiobooks on the go or enjoy narration as you read along, I have great news for you. You can download the audiobook version of *The Power of Sensitivity* for FREE just by signing up for a FREE 30-day Audible trial!

Visit: www.pristinepublish.com/audiobooks

YOUR FREE GIFT—
HEYOKA EMPATH

A lot of empaths feel trapped, as if they've hit a glass ceiling that they can't penetrate. They know there's another level to their gift, but they can't seem to figure out what it is. They've read dozens of books, been to counseling, and confided in other experienced empaths, but that glass ceiling remains. They feel alone and alienated from the rest of the world, because they know they've got so much more to give but can't access it. Does this sound like you?

The inability to connect to your true and authentic self is a tragedy. Being unable to embrace the full extent of your humanity is a terrible misfortune. The driving force of human nature is to live according to one's own sense of self, values, and emotions. Since the beginning of time, philosophers, writers, and scholars have argued that authenticity is one of the most important elements of an individual's well-being.

When there's a disconnect between a person's inner being and their expressions, it can be psychologically damaging. Heyokas are the most powerful type of empaths, and many of them are not fully aware of who they are. While other empaths experience feelings of overwhelm and exhaustion from absorbing others' energy and emotions, heyoka empaths experience an additional aspect of exhaustion in that they are fighting a constant battle with their inability to be completely authentic.

The good news is that the only thing stopping you from becoming your authentic self is a lack of knowledge. You need to know exactly who you are so you can tap into the resources that have been lying dormant within you. In this bonus e-book, you'll gain in-depth information about the seven signs that you're a heyoka empath, and why certain related abilities are such powerful traits. You'll find many of the answers you've been searching for your entire life such as:

- Why you feel uncomfortable when you're around certain people
- How you always seem to find yourself on the right path even though your decisions are not based on logic or rationale
- The reason you get so offended when you find out others have lied to you
- Why you analyze everything in such detail
- The reason why humor is such an important part of your life
- Why you refuse to follow the crowd, regardless of the consequences
- The reason why strangers and animals are drawn to you.

There are three main components to authenticity: understanding who you are, expressing who you are, and letting the world experience who you are. Your first step on this journey is to know who you are, and with these seven signs that you're a heyoka empath, you'll find out. I've included snippets about the first three signs in this description to give you confidence that you're on the right track:

Sign 1: You Feel and Understand Energy

Heyoka empaths possess a natural ability to tap into energy. They can walk into a room and immediately discern the atmosphere. When an individual walks past them, they can literally see into their soul because they can sense the aura that person is carrying. But empaths also understand their own energy, and they allow it to guide them. You will often hear this ability referred to as "the sixth sense." The general consensus is that only a few people have this gift. But the reality is that everyone was born with the ability to feel energy; it's just been demonized and turned into something spooky, when in actual fact, it's the most natural state to operate in.

Sign 2: You Are Led by Your Intuition

Do you find that you just know things? You don't spend hours, days, and weeks agonizing over decisions—you can just feel that something is the right thing to do, and you go ahead and do it. That's because you're led by your intuition, and you're connected to the deepest part of yourself. You know your soul, you listen to it, and you trust it. People like Oprah Winfrey, Steve Jobs and Richard Branson followed their intuition steadfastly, and it led them to become some of the most successful people in the history of the world. Living from within is the way we were created to be, and those who trust this ability will find their footing in life a lot more quickly than others. Think of it as a GPS system—when it's been programmed properly, it will always take you to your destination via the fastest route.

Sign 3: You Believe in Complete Honesty

In general, empaths don't like being around negative energy, and there's nothing that can shift a positive frequency faster than dishonesty. Anything that isn't the truth is a lie, even the tiny ones that we excuse away as "white lies." And as soon as they're released from someone's mouth, so is negative energy. Living an authentic life requires complete honesty at all times, and although the truth may hurt, it's better than not being able to trust someone. Heyoka empaths get very uncomfortable in the presence of liars. They are fully aware that the vibrations of the person don't match the words they are saying. Have you ever experienced a brain freeze mid-conversation? All of a sudden you just couldn't think straight, you couldn't articulate yourself properly, and things just got really awkward? That's because your empath antenna picked up on a lie.

Heyoka Empath: 7 Signs You're a Heyoka Empath & Why It's So Powerful is a revolutionary tool that will help you transition from uncertainty to complete confidence in who you are. In this easy-to-read guide, I will walk you through exactly what makes you a heyoka empath. I've done the research for you—so you'll no longer need to spend hours, days, weeks, and even years searching for answers, because everything you need is right here in this book.

You have a deep need to share yourself with the world, but you've been too afraid because you knew something was missing. The information within this book is the missing piece in the jigsaw puzzle of your life. There's no turning back now!

Get *Heyoka Empath* for Free by Visiting

www.pristinepublish.com/empathbonus

CHAPTER 1:

THE HIGHLY SENSITIVE PERSON—TRAITS AND CHARACTERISTICS

For as long as I can remember, I've struggled with strong smells, bright lights, and loud noises. I was super sensitive to emotions, and channeled into what people were feeling before they'd said anything about it. Throughout my life, I've been called a witch, a psychic, a weirdo—and everything else but highly sensitive. I am also very creative. Writing is my passion, and I can also draw and play musical instruments, despite never having had any training.

In school, my teachers were constantly calling my parents to discuss my inability to concentrate. I barely passed high school, and was written off as being lazy and unambitious. I was often scolded and punished at home for being "too emotional," or "over the top." When I found out I was highly sensitive and I started talking about it with my mother, things started to make sense to her. She would tell me stories of how, between the ages of two to six, I would scream and cry when certain people came to the house. When I got old enough to talk, I'd tell my parents outright that I didn't like certain people. When I was asked why, I would say, "I don't know, I just don't." I didn't know it at the time, but I was sensing their negative energy. My way of dealing with my awkwardness was to become an introvert. I had no idea I was highly sensitive. In this chapter, I'm going to talk about the traits and characteristics of highly sensitive people. But I want to start by saying that highly sensitive people are not necessarily empaths.

The Difference Between Highly Sensitive People and Empaths

Empaths and highly sensitive people share similar traits. These include high empathy, sensitivity to smell, sound, and light, as well as needing to spend time alone, difficulty being in groups of people, and a low threshold for stimulation. Also, highly sensitive people take longer to relax after a hectic day because their nervous systems work slower in this regard. In general, HSPs are introverts, whereas empaths have the capacity to be introverts or extroverts, even though they are also typically introverts. Empaths and HSPs share a love for quiet environments, nature, an introspective inner life, and a strong desire to be of service to others.

You could say that empaths are the extreme version of highly sensitive people. They sense energy, even if it's very slight, and they absorb it from people and environments into their own bodies. Highly sensitive people don't have this ability. Empaths who don't understand their gift find it difficult to distinguish between their emotions and the emotions of others. They also have regular supernatural encounters, and can communicate directly with nature, animals, and their spirit guides. It is also important to note that you can be an empath and an HSP at the same time, but as you have read, these personality traits are not the same.

What is High Sensitivity?

When a person's nervous system is sensitive to emotional, physical, or social stimuli, it is referred to as "high sensitivity." In medical circles, you will also hear it called "sensory processing sensitivity." The term was pioneered in the mid-1990s by psychologists Elaine and Arthur Aron, and since then it has increased in popularity. If you've been told, *"You think too much,"* or, *"You're too sensitive,"* there is a high chance you are an HSP. But before you make that judgment call, here are some character traits that experts have agreed are specific to highly sensitive people:

- Your inner life is deep and complex; you have strong thoughts and feelings.
- You need to relax in a dark, quiet room after a busy day.
- You are overwhelmed by sensory stimuli such as bright lights, noisy crowds, or uncomfortable clothing.
- You experience deep emotions when exposed to beauty expressed through nature, art, or the human spirit.
- You avoid watching anything violent because it distresses you.

How High Sensitivity Impacts Your Life

Before I knew I was highly sensitive, I thought my life was cursed. I was very familiar with the negative effects of high sensitivity, and I hated waking up in the mornings because I knew

I would have to deal with something distressing. So I'm going to start with some of the negative effects of the personality trait:

You Can't Say No: Highly sensitive people often become enslaved to other people's expectations because they don't like disappointing them, and as a result will say yes to every request. One of the main reasons for this is that you can sense feelings of disappointment in others. There's absolutely nothing wrong with wanting to help out your friends, but what happens is that you end up overwhelmed because you've got too much to do. Overwhelm then leads to stress and anxiety, which highly sensitive people find even more difficult to deal with.

Tolerations: Tolerations are the things or people in our daily lives that drain our energy. They are unnecessary distractions that we tolerate because they've just become a part of our life—but things would be much better if they were not there. Distractions are particularly frustrating to highly sensitive people when they are trying to concentrate. If they work from home, for example, and have children or siblings who keep disrupting their flow, this will cause them more disruption than it would the average person.

Stress from Conflicts: Highly sensitive people don't like conflicts and will avoid them at all costs. The problem is that they can sense when someone has an issue with them even if the person doesn't say it. The highly sensitive person will agonize over the situation, going over incidents in their head, trying to work out when the offense was caused. This can lead to misinterpretations and can create an uncomfortable environment for the highly sensitive person.

Personal Failures: Failure is the highly sensitive person's worst nightmare; they are perfectionists and hate the idea of being substandard. As a result, they procrastinate on projects or will stop partway through if they get any sort of negative criticism. HSPs don't like being evaluated or watched, especially when they're doing something they consider challenging. An embarrassing moment like experiencing stage fright in the middle of a speech will live with the highly sensitive person long after the event, whereas the average person will have forgotten about it in a day or two.

Emotional Overload: Emotional overload is when your feelings become so intense that you have difficulty managing them. Highly sensitive people are typically overwhelmed by negative emotions such as guilt, fear, or anger. It's easier for the average person to manage their emotions because they don't experience them as intensely as HSPs.

Depression: Aside from the chemical and biological reasons for depression, a lot of people are prone to it because of negative thinking. Your thoughts control your emotions, so when your mind is preoccupied with all the bad things that are going on in your life, you are going to feel depressed. Highly sensitive people are more prone to depressive episodes because they process things on a deeper level—and that includes their thoughts; they have the tendency to get lost in them. This is combined with the fact that they feel things more deeply, which compounds the problem.

Anxiety: Like depression, anxiety starts in the mind, but the difference is that anxiety is triggered by a fear of the future, worry, and concern about what might go wrong. When you're facing a difficult situation, anxiety will make you want to escape from it.

Again, highly sensitive people are prone to anxiety because they are overthinkers, and when these thoughts are negative, it's easy to become anxious.

Affected by Negative Energy: The average person can walk into a room and sense that the atmosphere isn't right, but it won't necessarily affect them. This is not the case with highly sensitive people. They sense negative energy so deeply that it drains them. After being in a negative environment, highly sensitive people feel tired and heavy. I used to sleep for 16-20 hours after being affected by negative energy.

This doesn't sound good, does it? It appears that there are way too many negative traits associated with high sensitivity. But while highly sensitive people have a lot to deal with, the advantages far outweigh the disadvantages once you know how to manage them (we'll get into that later). Let's take a look at some of the awesome benefits associated with being highly sensitive:

A High Level of Self-Awareness: Highly sensitive people are far from confused about who they are. We are so tuned in to our own souls that it's difficult to lead us in a direction we know we are not supposed to go in. Not only do we understand our own emotions, we understand other people's emotions and how to react to them. We know we're different, and we understand that people don't feel things on the same level as us, but that doesn't mean that our feelings are not valid. We find it easy to identify our emotional triggers, which helps us stay away from things that can be damaging.

Natural Nurturers: Highly sensitive people have a strong desire to nurture others, and because it comes naturally to us, we do so very well. We make people feel comfortable, heard, seen and acknowledged. When our loved ones are in pain, we desperately want to see them happy and healthy again, and we will do whatever it takes to help them get there.

We Experience Feelings Deeply: Highly sensitive people find meaning in everything; nothing goes unnoticed with us. We experience the world with heightened emotions. Witnessing flowers bloom doesn't usually trigger strong emotions in people. But the highly sensitive person will see it as a beautiful expression of nature, and will experience great joy because of it. I have always grown plants in my house, and when I see the seeds starting to sprout, I get very emotional—it's absolutely amazing to me.

High Empathy: Because we can sense emotions, we find it easy to put ourselves in other people's shoes. We can't help this; it's automatic. Highly sensitive people connect with the world through our emotions, and this makes us good listeners. Because we can sense what others are feeling, we take it seriously when someone is going through emotional turmoil. Where others would dismiss what someone is trying to communicate, the HSP will listen intently because we can actually *feel* what they are saying. While the average person might offer practical advice on how to quickly get over the problem, highly sensitive people see the benefit in allowing people to express themselves in a way that enables them to release their emotions.

Self-Care Experts: Highly sensitive people understand how they are affected by their environment, whether it be an untidy house, negative energy from friends and family members, or everyday happenings that we find overwhelming. We are lovers of peace and harmony, and we wish that everyone in the world could just get along, but that's an ideal we know will never happen. To protect ourselves from the harsh realities of life, we find ways to self-soothe and keep the flame of our soul burning so we can continue being a light in dark places. We quickly learn how important it is to be gentle with ourselves and to take care of our inner being.

Grateful for the Small Things: It doesn't take much to impress highly sensitive people because we find pleasure in the small things. A romantic gesture such as a back rub, or a stroke of the face, or a handwritten love note can elicit feelings of euphoria for us. Hearing a song connected to an important time in my life can instantly transport me back to that moment and flood me with the same emotions. The highly sensitive person's inner child is alive and well.

A True Sense of Purpose: Although highly sensitive people don't like pain and would rather avoid it at all costs, when we do go through adversity, we have the ability to find purpose in the struggle in a way that most people don't. We find treasure in dark emotions such as sadness, and in many ways it nourishes our soul. Highly sensitive people understand that in order to experience humanity in its fullness, we must embrace both negative and positive experiences and emotions. Because we understand that there are benefits in tribulation, we can use our pain to water the parched souls of others, and this is where we find purpose.

Close Relationships: Highly sensitive people bond very quickly with the right people. We know who to open the door of our hearts to, and who to close it to. Humans crave authenticity; we want to be around people with whom we can be ourselves, and who bring out the best in us. Highly sensitive people know how to tap into the core of the human soul. They can find that place that's like a well of living water, the place that flows with the rhythm of life. When you find people like this, you don't want to let them go.

Now you know what you've got to look forward to, it's time to start making the necessary changes in your life so you can take full advantage of being a highly sensitive person.

CHAPTER 2:

HOW TO SET UP YOUR HOME ENVIRONMENT

Living environment is crucial for highly sensitive people, and the nature of this personality trait can make it very difficult to have roommates or to live in a family home. Sometimes, however, you have no control over where you live, so you've got to make the best out of a bad situation. When I discovered I was highly sensitive, and started reading about coping strategies, the first thing I did was rearrange my house. It had an immediate positive effect on my emotional state. Here are some tips on how to set up your home environment:

Bedroom Arrangement

If you live at home with your parents and siblings, or you've got roommates, your bedroom is the safest place for you. Even if you have nighttime anxiety or light sensitivities, these suggestions will ensure you always get the best possible night's sleep.

- **Eliminate Clutter:** Start by getting rid of anything you haven't used in over a year. Either throw these items out or give them to a charity shop. If you have a desk in your room, invest in baskets, folders, and drawers in which to store paperwork and stationery. Keep only the bare necessities such as your computer on your desk.

- **Decorate with Neutral Colors:** Shades of tan, cream, or gray work well for the bedroom. To make the decor pop, add accents of green or blue. These combinations invoke feelings of peace and calm.

- **Separate Sleep and Work:** If you need to work in your bedroom, place a curtain or screen between your bed and desk. This way, you create a clear separation between work and rest.

- **Your Bedding:** A good mattress, or a high-quality topper, and a comfy duvet and pillow will drastically improve your sleep.

- **Blackout Curtains:** Light exposure has a negative effect on sleep quality. Blackout curtains will create a barrier against morning sunlight and keep the room dark to create a more sleep-friendly environment.

LIVING ROOM ARRANGEMENT

If you don't live alone, you will need to have a conversation with the people you live with before you start moving things around and redecorating. The living room is generally the most visited room in the house; whether you spend your time curled up on the sofa reading a good book or watching your favorite TV shows, you need to create an environment that benefits you. The following ideas will help you construct the perfect HSP-friendly living room:

- **Photos:** Keep framed photos of friends, family, and loved ones around your living room. This helps you feel connected to the people closest to you and creates a sense of consistency because you get to see them every time you're in the room.

- **Fresh Flowers:** Not only do fresh flowers look beautiful, they also have a positive effect on our moods and health, and help to boost productivity.

- **Add Soft Blankets and Pillows:** Adding them to your couch and armchairs will add extra comfort to your seating area.

- **White Candles:** Arrange white candles on your coffee tables, side tables and fireplace mantels. Lighting them during the evening hours creates a warm, glowing atmosphere. If you are sensitive to strong smells, be sure to get fragrance-free candles.

BATHROOM ARRANGEMENT

Whether you have a tiny space or a large, luxurious bathroom, adapt it to meet your needs. Again, if you live with other people, ask permission first.

- **Natural Muted Lights:** You might live in an apartment where there is no window in the bathroom. If so, buy yourself a sunlight lamp. It gives off the same light that you would get from natural sunlight.

- **Shower Head:** Enjoy a more soothing and satisfying shower experience with a rain shower head. It emulates the feeling of rainwater.

- **Bathrobes and Towels:** If you suffer from skin sensitivities, invest in some high-quality towels and bathrobes. For the softest touch, look for microfiber, pure or Egyptian cotton.

- **Waterproof Speaker:** Listen to relaxing spa or motivational music while you get ready to start your day. A study reported in the *Stanford News* found that listening to empowering music is just as effective as medication in its ability to change the function of the brain.

- **Essential Oils:** Keep a selection of essential oils in the bathroom and add a few drops to your bathwater for an aromatherapy effect. If you don't have a bath, put a few drops on the floor of your shower. The hot water will activate the smell and provide the same experience as a bath.

Kitchen Arrangement

Whether you prefer cooking or ordering takeout, it's important to organize and structure your kitchen in a way that will keep it functional, decluttered, and calm.

- **Kitchen Appliances:** If you are sensitive to sound, purchase sound-sensitive kitchen appliances.

- **Sound-Dampening Pads:** The sound of doors and drawers slamming can trigger anxiety in highly sensitive people. Sound-dampening pads will drown out the noise.

- **Light Replacement:** Highly sensitive people often have an aversion to harsh lighting. Use warmer LED bulbs and, if possible, install dimmer switches so you have full control of the ambience in your kitchen.

- **Air Purifier:** An air purifier near the trash will get rid of any smells and keep the atmosphere fresh.

- **Draw Dividers and Organizers:** To maintain a sense of neatness and harmony, keep everything in its rightful place by using organizers and dividers.

Home Office Space

Working from home is ideal for highly sensitive people, but keeping your office space well organized is essential. HSPs who are sensitive to distractions and sound will need to modify their work environment to maximize their productivity.

- **Fidget Cube:** I work from home, and this was a game changer for me. As you are no doubt aware, highly sensitive people are easily distracted, especially during meetings, brainstorming activities, and presentations. To keep your mind focused on the task, you need to channel that distracted energy into something else, and a fidget cube is ideal.

- **Limit Artificial Light:** Use sheer curtains for your windows to allow more natural light into the room, or just remove the curtains. Sunshine has many health benefits including better sleep, reduced stress, and improved mental health. It also works as a natural energy booster, which will increase your focus during the day.

- **Bullet Journal or Calendar:** It's easy to get overwhelmed by the amount of work you have to do. Reduce the anxiety associated with having too much to do by organizing your tasks with a calendar or bullet journal. I feel at my best when my entire day is planned out in front of me, including the time I'm going to take breaks, have lunch, and anything else I need to do throughout the day. An established daily routine provides consistency and order, which research suggests improves your memory and mental health.

- **Noise-Canceling Headphones:** Random noises like the neighbors opening and shutting doors, the mailman, traffic, and anything else that goes on outside your office space can throw you off track. Once your mind gets distracted, it can be difficult to get back into flow mode. Prevent this by investing in some noise-canceling headphones and listening to motivational music while you work.

- **Ergonomic Office Chair:** Office supplies that help you work on your posture will maximize your comfort levels throughout the day. Invest in supplies such as lumbar support pillows, wrist rests, and cushioned mouse pads.

Embrace Minimalism

Fix me! I'm broken! I don't belong here! Tidy me up! Clean me! Put me away! That was what I heard every time I walked through my cluttered home. Before I started on my minimalism journey, my house was a mess—full of clothes I didn't wear, paperwork I didn't need, and old equipment packed in boxes. The home that should have been my safe haven was a major source of anxiety because everything was so chaotic. There was no order in my environment, and it had a terrible effect on my mental health.

When I walked through my house, my eyes zeroed in on all the unfinished chores, like clothes that needed washing or folding, thirsty plants, and dishes piled up in the sink. Or I would focus on the mismatched decorations, the frayed carpet, or the loose screw on the shelf. Everything that needed doing was constantly on my radar, and it left me drained and exhausted.

For highly sensitive people, a crowded house can become a source of stress, anxiety and fatigue. I didn't understand that minimalism was what I needed in my life until I put it into practice. There are some very distinct reasons why highly sensitive people need minimalism. Here are some of them:

Minimalism Allows You to be Authentic: Society does not cater to highly sensitive people. Western culture thrives on *more is better*—we are sold bigger, better, faster, and newer. Life is all about hustling to gain more possessions, and there is no end in sight. A lot of the time, HSPs just don't feel like they fit in to a world that leaves them totally depleted. They feel like running away from career or social opportunities that demand too much. Often, the HSP's only defense mechanism against mental torment is loneliness and isolation. When you know what you can and cannot tolerate as a highly sensitive person, you can use minimalism to cut out the activities, clutter and relationships that drain your energy. In this way, you make room for the things that bring you the greatest joy, even if they don't conform to the norms of the society we are living in.

Minimalism Helps You Set Your Priorities: When your priorities are in order, and you take care of those things first, you eliminate the nonessentials, which often cause the most distress. When you start cutting things out, you will begin asking yourself questions such as:

- Will this opportunity, event, person or job bring me joy?
- What do I value?

- What will add value to my life?
- What things are most important to me?
- What are my major goals?
- What do I need, to bring me true happiness?

During this thought-provoking exercise, you will discover a deeper sense of self and determine what a meaningful life looks like to you. When you have your priorities in order, letting go of the things that don't benefit you will help enrich your life.

Your Home is Your Sanctuary

Highly sensitive people value a relaxing, calm and decluttered home. As I did, HSPs often start their minimalism journey by clearing out their living space. An environment that highlights your values and promotes a peaceful and serene atmosphere is ideal for highly sensitive people. When they've had a hard day at work or have been to a draining social event, HSPs take great comfort in coming home to a place that allows them to unwind and relax. Without a sanctuary, you will find it difficult to switch off. Here are some benefits of turning your living environment into a sanctuary:

You Can Tap Into Your Full Potential: As mentioned, decluttering isn't just about your home environment, but about every area of your life. To achieve your full potential as an HSP, you must have balance—and that comes by making sure your home, work, social, and love lives are all working in harmony; they must all be free from clutter. In this way, your mind is free to focus on and live out the things that will enable you to thrive.

It Creates an Inviting Atmosphere: I never allowed my friends and family to just turn up at my house; they had to give me notice—not only because I needed to make sure I was in the right frame of mind to have guests, but because my home was a constant mess. I was always so overwhelmed that I never got anything done. The sink was constantly full of dishes, the laundry was never organized, my bed was never made, and there were always clothes on the floor. My curtains were always drawn so that if anyone did stop by, they couldn't look through the window and tell whether I was in or not. There were plenty of times when I heard the doorbell ring, and I just wouldn't answer because there was no way I was letting anyone into my pigsty of a home. I was ashamed of it, and I knew I had to get it together—I just didn't know where to start. Now that my house is in order, everything is where it's supposed to be, and the energy and atmosphere is right, I have no problem having people over. I literally felt as if a huge black cloud had been removed from my home when I stopped living in chaos.

It Raises Your Energy Levels: Feng Shui has gained worldwide popularity in recent years. An Eastern practice focusing on the art of placement, it is based on the idea that the types of objects and the way they are placed in an environment has an effect on our energy. Even if you have no interest in Feng Shui, you are no doubt fully aware that you feel drained and disoriented when you are in a cluttered environment. I used to be such a hypocrite; if I went to visit someone and their house was untidy, I'd leave really quickly because it made me feel uncomfortable. I'd refuse any offer of food or drink, I wouldn't sit down, and my eyes would scan the room looking for creepy-crawlies. Untidy homes gave me the heebie-jeebies—yet I'd go right back to my own untidy house. I suppose the difference is that you're familiar with your own mess, but either way, it's not good for your energy. My vibrations went sky-high when I decluttered and minimized my home. I jumped out of bed every morning excited to start my day, I enjoyed standing in the kitchen making a cup of coffee, and every room in my house was comfortable and organized. I now feel very relaxed at home.

Now that you've got your house in order, you should feel a lot more comfortable in your surroundings. The next step is to get healthy, because a healthy body equals a healthy mind.

CHAPTER 3:

THE IMPORTANCE OF DIET AND EXERCISE

There is a strong connection between food and emotional well-being. Most people are unaware that inflammation in the body causes you to feel moody, tired, and irritable, and it has a negative effect on your sleep. When you get sick or injured, the body responds by triggering inflammation, which helps fight infection; once the infection has gone, the body stops producing inflammation. However, when we eat unhealthy food, don't get enough sleep, and experience stress, inflammation occurs—and research suggests that when it isn't fighting infection, inflammation can cause cardiovascular disease, autoimmune disease, cognitive issues, mood disorders, chronic fatigue and chronic pain.

Added sugar, simple carbs, and packaged and processed foods all increase inflammation and have a negative effect on the gut microbiome. The gut microbiome plays a critical role in digestion and the function of the immune system; it makes anti-inflammatory fatty acids, helps strengthen the gut barrier, and regulates mental well-being and mood. Your gut barrier is very important; when a gap develops, it causes leaky gut syndrome, and toxins and food particles leak into your bloodstream and gut, which contributes to inflammation. Stress, worry, nutrient-deficient foods, pain relievers and medications such as antibiotics all contribute to leaky gut.

Why Does This Affect Your Mood?

Emotions cause your gut and brain to communicate through signaling hormones and the vagus nerve. When your gut is imbalanced because of inflammation, stress, or leaky gut, the messages being communicated get mixed up, and it causes anxiety. For a highly sensitive person, this can be a recipe for disaster. Anxiety and overwhelm often cause you to binge-eat, which makes you feel even more overwhelmed, and it becomes a vicious downward spiral. The solution is to reduce inflammation through a Mediterranean diet and eating more probiotic and prebiotic vegetables to feed the good microbes in the gut. I started feeling better within two weeks of going on this diet.

The Mediterranean Diet

The Mediterranean diet consists of mainly plant foods. Foods grown in soil contain a wide variety of microbes. Organic food is best if you can afford it because the pesticides used to grow non-organic foods can trigger inflammation. Eat plenty of leeks, jicama, radishes, onion, heart artichokes, garlic and asparagus. These are inulin prebiotic vegetables that feed the good microbes. In addition, opt for fermented vegetables such as kimchee and sauerkraut. Pickles are also a good option. These all contain live probiotics that help restore healthy bacteria in the gut. You should also add more leafy green vegetables to your diet.

Avoid Packaged and Processed Foods: These include cookies, chips and cereals, as they are all packed with preservatives and additives that are harmful to the gut.

Omega 3 Oils: Stay away from hydrogenated and trans fats; pay attention to the ingredients on packaging and don't buy anything that says, "hydrogenated" on the ingredients label. Get rid of all safflower, sunflower, corn and canola oils. Avoid fast-food restaurants because they reuse already unhealthy oils. Replace the oils with vegetable fats from foods such as avocados and olives. Don't heat olive oil as it becomes rancid when cooked—use it for salad dressings instead. Avocado and coconut oils are good for cooking at high temperatures.

Lean Protein: Reduce your consumption of animal fat and animal protein because these also have a negative effect on the gut microbiome. Choose free-range options instead. At least one meal per day should be purely vegetarian, and you should make your meat portions as small as possible. Lean animal protein should come from protein sources other than pork and red meat. Consume more wild-caught fish, and, if you are not allergic to dairy, Greek yogurt.

Beans and Whole Grains: Whole grains strengthen your gut barrier, and the body digests them slower, which prevents blood-sugar spikes and keeps you full for longer. Opt for brown rice, quinoa, and sprouted whole-grain breads instead of breads made with refined flour. Soak whole grains such as rice and quinoa before cooking to make them easier to digest.

No Sugar: Added sugar and artificial sweeteners are all harmful for the gut. Bad bacteria feeds off sugar, which creates an imbalance where there is more bad than good bacteria in the gut. When my sweet tooth kicks in, I reach for high-quality dark chocolate. Studies also show that dark chocolate helps to relieve stress.

Why the Mediterranean Diet?

The Mediterranean diet protects the body against inflammation. Studies have also found that the diet improves mental well-being within 10 days. In 2015, *The Journal of Nutrition* reported that a group of women who participated in a study about the benefits of the Mediterranean diet experienced less confusion, improved memory and alertness, and increased contentment. In 2019, the journal *PLOS ONE* published a study which found that people who ate a Mediterranean diet for three weeks experienced less stress, less worry, and improved moods. The participants who did not change their diet and continued eating sugary foods and drinks, processed foods, and refined carbs continued to experience low moods.

A literature review of 21 studies conducted in 2017 found that a diet high in full-fat dairy, refined grains, sugary foods, and red meat contributes to low mood. On the other hand, a diet high in fish, vegetables, fruits, whole grains, olive oil, and less animal protein helped alleviate the feelings associated with low mood.

Additional Healthy Eating Advice

As a highly sensitive person, it's important that you are functioning at your best both physically and mentally in order to experience the full benefits of this personality trait. Food is your main source of energy, and there are some foods that will completely destroy your energy reserves. I've found that being disciplined about not putting them in my body makes a massive difference. Here are some of the main culprits:

Breakfast Cereals: Breakfast cereals – even the ones that are marketed as healthy, such as granola and instant oats – are packed with added sugar. Breakfast is considered the most important meal of the day because it boosts your energy, allowing you to power through your tasks. But breakfast cereals fail to achieve these results because they contain very little fiber, and as much as 50% of the total carbohydrates come from added sugar. The combination of low fiber and sugar spikes insulin and blood-sugar levels. The result is high energy followed by a crash shortly after. Additionally, research suggests that foods high in sugar make you crave more sugar! Now I understand why I always wanted something sweet by lunchtime after having a bowl of cereal in the morning.

White Rice, Bread and Pasta: Grains are a rich source of carbohydrates and provide the body with plenty of energy. But processed grains such as white rice, bread and pasta don't have the same effect. The fiber is stored in bran—the outer layer of the grain. During processing, this is removed, which lowers the level of fiber and causes it to be digested faster than whole grains. For this reason, a snack or a meal made from processed grains causes a quick rise in insulin and blood-sugar levels followed by an energy drop. Processed grains also lack another part of the grain called the "germ." The germ is rich in many nutrients such as B vitamins, which are required by the body to create energy.

Alcohol: I have always loved a Pina Colada on the rocks, but when I found out how alcohol depletes your energy, I stopped drinking it. One study found that people enjoy having a glass of alcohol with their evening meal because it helps them fall asleep. This sounds great, but it isn't. Research suggests that alcohol increases restlessness because it reduces the duration and quality of sleep. It drains your energy during the night, making you feel groggy in the morning.

However, research also highlights the fact that low to moderate levels of alcohol don't have the same negative effect on quality of sleep. Experts suggest consuming one glass per day for women, and two glasses per day for men.

Energy Drinks: The name is deceptive, and I am certain the manufacturers know exactly why they market them to us in this way. The assumption is that they increase your energy levels—and that is true. Studies have reported that they reduce sleepiness and boost memory and concentration by 24%. Energy drinks are made from a cocktail of stimulating ingredients. However, research has found that most of the energy-boosting effects come from caffeine and sugar.

With as many as 10 teaspoons per can, energy drinks contain alarmingly high amounts of sugar. They also contain more caffeine than the same quantity of coffee. The combination of caffeine and sugar causes a massive boost in energy, followed by a massive crash. Your response is to go and buy another energy drink—and the vicious cycle begins. In case you were thinking of replacing your energy drinks with coffee, it has the same effect, although milder. It is also important to mention that highly sensitive people are prone to anxiety, and due to their high caffeine content, energy drinks are known to cause anxiety, jitteriness, and heart palpitations. In rare cases, they can also cause panic attacks.

Fast and Fried Foods: I love fast and fried foods. I used to eat them all the time, especially when I was binge-eating. The greasier the better! I experienced massive satisfaction from eating them until the effects wore off. Fast and fried foods are low in fiber and high in fat, which slows down your digestion. When food is digested too slowly, it slows down the rate at which energy-boosting nutrients enter the body. While you are eating, your dopamine levels are going up, which is why you feel satisfied. Fried and fast foods are also low in the essential nutrients required to help boost energy levels. Due to the unhealthy ingredients, they make you feel extremely full, which zaps your energy, leaving you unable to do much of what you had planned.

Foods That Boost Your Energy

The afternoon slump is depressing because your performance is low, and highly sensitive people feel it the most. I used to get through my days by guzzling multiple cups of coffee and eating loads of sweet treats, which was a complete disaster. Once I started eating energy-sustaining and nutrient-rich foods, my days became a lot more productive. Here are some of my favorite foods and snacks:

Salmon: Salmon is one of the few natural food sources that provide vitamin D. One of the benefits of vitamin D is that it helps you beat fatigue by energizing the body. Salmon is also high in B vitamins, especially B12, which plays an important role in maintaining high energy.

Greek Yogurt: Make sure any Greek yogurt you purchase is natural, with no added sugar. For a tasty snack, combine it with chopped almonds and fresh fruit. It is high in protein, which helps sustain your energy levels.

Steel-Cut Oats: Rolled oats are good, but you will get more benefits from steel-cut oats. They don't go through the same process as rolled oats, which means they retain more protein and fiber.

Cottage Cheese: There are 25 grams of protein in one cup of cottage cheese. Spread it over some crackers for a quick afternoon snack.

Almonds: A small handful of almonds will give you an instant energy boost because they are high in fiber, protein and heart-healthy fats. They are also packed with vitamins and minerals such as magnesium, riboflavin, copper, and manganese, which help with the energy production process.

Tuna: Top whole-wheat crackers or bread with some tuna—the combination of protein and fat will give you an instant pick-me-up.

Dark Chocolate: Aim for dark chocolate that contains at least 75% cacao. Cacao is high in flavanols, which improves blood flow to the brain.

Ricotta on Whole-Wheat Bread: Fiber and protein not only keep you full for longer, they also give you plenty of energy.

Avocado: Packed with healthy fats and fiber, avocado is digested slowly, providing you with a sustainable energy source.

Eggs: Starting your day with eggs or having a hard-boiled egg as a snack provides long-lasting energy. Eggs are full of healthy protein and fats. They are also versatile and can be eaten for breakfast, lunch, or dinner.

Quinoa: All grains contain protein, but quinoa has the highest amount. It is a natural carbohydrate, and it's packed with energy-boosting nutrients such as manganese, magnesium, and folate.

Sweet Potatoes: I absolutely love sweet potatoes; they contain complex carbohydrates and protein, which is the perfect combination for long-lasting energy.

Walnuts: High in omega-3 fatty acids, they will keep you energized and satisfied.

Watery Foods: Dehydration causes a lack of energy. There are plenty of foods that not only have a high water content but also provide the nutrients required for energy maintenance. Watery foods include cucumbers, melon, berries, citrus fruits, and fresh herbs.

Trail Mix: Instead of buying trail mix from the store, make your own because it won't contain the extra sugar found in the store-bought version. Combine dried cherries or cranberries with raw almonds and dark-chocolate chips. If you feel like a more savory mix, combine sunflower seeds, soy nuts and pumpkin seeds with a pinch of cayenne pepper, onion powder, and garlic powder.

Hummus: Hummus is a very popular Middle Eastern spread and dip made by blending garlic, lemon juice, olive oil, ground sesame seeds, tahini and chickpeas. It is high in plant-based protein and fiber.

Bananas: Bananas are a powerful source of vitamin B6, potassium, and complex carbohydrates, all of which help boost energy levels.

Smoothies: How much energy you get from your smoothies will depend on what you put in them. I find that flax seeds, protein powder, banana, peanut butter and milk work wonders. Also consider chia seeds, kefir, blackberries, blueberries and strawberries.

Spinach: A serve of spinach provides you with your daily magnesium intake, which helps the body produce energy. Spinach is also high in folate, which helps the body turn food into energy. Additionally, it keeps your body in an alkaline state, which gives you more energy.

Apple and String Cheese: One stick of string cheese provides 6.7 grams of protein. Combined with an apple, which is a good source of carbohydrates, antioxidants and vitamin C, you will have plenty of energy to get you through the day.

Beans/Legumes: Edamame, kidney, black beans, lentils, and garbanzo beans are all high in fiber and plant-based protein. They make the perfect energy-boosting lunch.

Maca: Maca is a plant that originates from Peru; it is highly nutritious, containing manganese, vitamin B6, potassium and iron, all of which are great for boosting energy. Maca is most popular in powdered form. You can add it to oats, smoothies, herbal tea, or any other hot beverage.

Sliced Turkey: Turkey is a nutrient-dense protein containing minerals such as potassium, magnesium, phosphorous, selenium and vitamin B12, all of which are necessary for energy production.

Exercise as a Form of Stress Relief

We can't escape from stress—it's a normal part of life. According to the Anxiety and Depression Association of America, seven out of ten American adults experience stress or anxiety every day, and the majority state that it has a negative effect on their lives. One survey reported that many people experience emotional and physical symptoms because of stress.

Although you can't eliminate stress, you can learn to manage it, and studies suggest that the majority of people manage to do so. In an online poll by ADAA, people reported that they use exercise, listening to music and talking to friends to cope with stress.

Highly sensitive people experience stress and anxiety on a much deeper level than the average person. It is therefore extremely important to have an effective outlet, and exercise is a great way to relieve the overwhelm that HSPs are subjected to every day. Regular exercise can help relieve mild depression, anger, and anxiety, and it can also improve mood and sleep quality.

The Benefits of Exercise

Regular aerobic exercise has a remarkable ability to relax and exhilarate, providing calmness and stimulation, which reduce the symptoms associated with stress and depression. Endurance athletes are no strangers to these benefits, and several studies have verified that exercise is an effective treatment for clinical depression and anxiety disorders. The mental benefits of exercise are neurochemical: It stimulates the production of the feel-good hormone and natural painkiller endorphins. You will often hear athletes talk about the "runner's high"—the feeling of optimism and relaxation experienced after a long run. Endorphins cancel out stress hormones such as cortisol and adrenaline.

The emotional benefits of exercise are also increased because as you lose weight and increase your strength and stamina, your self-esteem will improve. You'll gain a sense of control and mastery, of self-confidence and pride. This renewed energy and vigor will help you succeed in many areas of life. The discipline of consistent exercise will motivate you to achieve the important life goals you've set for yourself.

Sports and exercise also provide you with opportunities to escape from the things in life that are causing you worry and keeping you distracted. When the body is busy, the mind is occupied with the task at hand. The following are the three main types of exercise you should focus on:

Strength Training: Contrary to popular belief, strength training isn't about powerlifting and bulking up. One of the reasons I used to hate working out with weights was because it involved fighting to use the weight machines at the gym! I've lost count of the number of times I've walked out because of this. If this is a problem for you, you might want to consider the following:

- **Use Weights at Home:** A quick Google search will tell you where to buy them.

- **Strength-Training Videos:** YouTube will provide you with a good choice of experts offering step-by-step instructions on how to improve your strength at home.

- **Download Apps:** There are plenty of apps that will provide you with strength-training guides.

- **A Personal Trainer:** Most people are put off this option because a personal trainer is not cheap. However, they usually have their own gyms and provide one-on-one training.

Cardiovascular Exercise: Cardiovascular exercise keeps the heart muscle strong and speeds up the fat-burning process. It is also very helpful for highly sensitive people because it boosts endorphin production and helps get rid of cortisol. For HSPs, cardio gets rid of the tension and replaces it with a sense of grounding and strength. Cardio is another type of exercise I detested at the gym because I found the instructors to be over the top and annoying. I also saw the machines as glorified hamster wheels. So here are some ideas to get a good cardio workout:

- HSPs love being out in nature, so a run or a brisk walk through the park works well. Whatever outdoor spaces you enjoy the most, take your walk there.

- If you want to go to a group class but can't deal with all the extras, take a cardio-yoga class. The environment is more chilled and relaxed, and you will get the same benefits as any other cardio class without feeling overwhelmed.

- If you prefer to work out at home, there are plenty of apps and videos that will provide you with instructions for the perfect cardio workout.

- Link cardio with something you enjoy such as reading. Download audiobooks and read as you walk/run.

Flexibility: Men usually scoff at the idea of flexibility training because they believe it's too feminine. But the reality is that anyone can participate in flexibility training for increased versatility of movement and mobility. Here are some of the best ways to bend:

- **Dynamic Stretches:** This is a more intense form of stretching that involves exercises such as trunk rotations and bodyweight lunges. Dynamic stretches can also include low-impact exercises such as jogging, rope jumping, shuttle runs, and agility drills.

- **Stagnant Stretches:** Think middle school P.E. class! Stagnant stretching involves slowly lengthening the muscle and holding the pose for 30 seconds. A stagnant stretch might include the classic hamstring stretch or side bends. The aim is to release tension, which makes the muscles more pliable and less susceptible to strains and pulls.

- **Yoga:** Yoga is a great way to incorporate flexibility into your exercise routine. It helps with strength and balance as well as mobility. If you feel comfortable, join a yoga class at your local gym, or take classes online.

STRESS RELIEF AND AUTOREGULATION EXERCISE

Stress comes in different forms and causes a variety of symptoms. Mental symptoms include panic, sensations of dread and foreboding, hostility, anger, insomnia, restlessness, irritability, and worry. Mental stress can trigger physical symptoms such as tense muscles that cause back and neck pain, headaches, taut facial expressions, and the inability to sit still. Physical symptoms can also include unquenchable thirst and the feeling of a lump in the throat that makes it difficult to swallow. The skin can become clammy, sweaty and pale; intestinal symptoms can manifest in the form of diarrhea, cramps, heartburn or butterflies. You might also experience frequent urination, tingling in the fingers and face, chest tightness, rapid breathing, and a strong pulse. Some rare physical symptoms include nonstop coughing or sighing. More severe symptoms include lightheadedness and fainting.

The physical symptoms of stress are upsetting and cause additional mental stress, which creates a vicious cycle of anxiety and tension. As a highly sensitive person, you need to remove the triggers in your life that cause stress, but you should also involve physical activity and autoregulation exercises as these will be of significant benefit to you.

Autoregulation exercises are techniques that help replace the downward spiral of stress with a cycle of response. These include:

Breathing Exercises: Rapid, erratic and shallow breathing is a common stress response. Deep, slow and regular breathing lets the body know that it's in a relaxed state. The following exercise will help you control your breathing to calm your body down:

- Slowly take a deep breath and push your stomach out to maximize the use of your diaphragm.

- Hold your breath for a couple of seconds.

- Breathe out slowly and think to yourself, "Relax."

- Repeat the exercise 10 times and keep your focus on slow, deep breathing.

- Practice this breathing exercise at least twice a day.

Mental Exercises: Mental exercises help calm the mind, which can allow you to get a better understanding of the issues that are causing you stress, and help you relax. Mental exercises include journaling, talking therapy and meditation.

Meditation: Meditation encourages focused attention and a heightened state of awareness. It has been practiced in different cultures and religions for centuries. Studies suggest that there are several psychological benefits to meditation such as promoting a sense of peace, calm, and emotional well-being.

- Choose a time and a place that is free from noise and distraction. A slightly dark room is most effective. If you can, wait at least two hours after eating and use the bathroom before getting started.

- Choose a mantra such as, "I am calm and peaceful," or, "I am relaxed and happy."

- Sit in a comfortable position and start taking deep, slow breaths. Focus your mind on your breath.

- Close your eyes to achieve a passive, relaxed state of mind.

- Start repeating your mantra, either out loud or in your head.

- Practice meditating twice a day for five minutes at a time, increasing the time by five-minute increments as you get used to it.

Progressive Muscle Relaxation: Stressed muscles are tense and tight. When the muscles are relaxed, it is easier to release stress from the body. Progressive muscle relaxation takes some time to get right, but it's worth putting the effort in because it is very beneficial. It is best to either listen to instructions on a video or have someone read them out to you, because they are quite extensive and you probably won't remember them.

The technique focuses on the major muscle groups and involves tightening each muscle, holding the squeeze for 20 seconds, and then releasing it slowly. Focus on the tension being released as the muscle relaxes. The instructions are as follows:

- Arch your eyebrows and wrinkle your forehead. Hold for 20 seconds and relax.

- Squeeze your eyes shut tight. Hold for 20 seconds and relax.

- Flare your nostrils and crease your nose. Hold for 20 seconds and relax.

- Firmly push your tongue against the roof of your mouth. Hold for 20 seconds and relax.

- Squeeze all your facial features together. Hold for 20 seconds and relax.

- Tightly clench your jaws. Hold for 20 seconds and relax.

- Pull your chin to your chest to tense your neck. Hold for 20 seconds and relax.

- Bend your back by pushing your stomach forwards. Hold for 20 seconds and relax.

- Take a very deep breath in. Hold for 20 seconds and relax.

- Clench your thigh and buttock muscles. Hold for 20 seconds and relax.

- Squeeze your biceps. Hold for 20 seconds and relax.
- Clench your fists and tense your arms. Hold for 20 seconds and relax.
- Press your feet into the floor. Hold for 20 seconds and relax.
- Push your toes upwards. Hold for 20 seconds and relax.

The routine should take around 15 minutes. Practice it twice a day.

Talking Therapy: Not everyone can afford to see a therapist—although obviously that is the ideal scenario as a therapist will be able to give you professional insight into what you're going through. However, if you can't afford it, speak to a close friend, relative, co-worker, or anyone else you trust. Talking therapy involves having an open and honest discussion about the problems that are causing you distress. The person you are speaking to can provide a different perspective on your issues and perhaps help you come up with strategies to manage or overcome them. According to the American Psychological Association, approximately 75% of people who use talking therapy experience benefits. These include:

- A feeling of empowerment
- Improved communication skills
- New insights about your life
- The ability to make choices that will benefit you
- Developing coping strategies to help you work through your problems

Journaling: Since I'm a writer, I love journaling. It helps me acknowledge my feelings so I am able to better manage stress. Every Monday evening, I use the following ten journal prompts. They help me shift my focus to the things I can control instead of worrying about what I can't. The prompts also give me some direction in terms of what action to take. I find that once I have a plan in place and I know what I need to do, I'm a lot less stressed. Here are my prompts and some of my actual responses:

- **What situation/s are causing you to feel stressed?** *I am going back to work on Monday; I'm scared there will be new people in the office.*

- **What's your reason for being afraid?** *I am scared they won't like me and think I'm weird. I'm also afraid they might have negative energy and overwhelm me with it.*

- **In which area of your body do you feel the stress?** *My brain is all over the place. My shoulders and chest are tight.*

- **What is your breathing pattern like?** *I am taking quick, shallow breaths. Sometimes I feel as if I can't breathe.*

- **What underlying belief is contributing to the stress?** *The belief that the new colleagues will team up with my old work colleagues to talk about how weird I am.*

- **Is this fear familiar?** *Yes—I feel it every time I'm about to enter a new environment. I also feel it when I'm going to a social gathering with people I know. My fear is always that I won't be accepted because I don't act like everyone else.*

- **What else is your worry telling you?** *That I'm putting too much pressure on myself to be liked. I expect perfection all the time, and I get nervous because, deep down, I know that perfection is impossible to achieve.*

- **Have you been in a situation like this before?** *I believe I have felt people's negative energy towards me for being weird. It's almost like I could read their mind.*

- **What lessons can you apply from those situations?** *That I didn't have any actual evidence that people didn't like me because I was weird, since I didn't hear them say anything.*

- **What adjustments or action do you need to take?** *I can't control whether there are going to be new people in the office. To prepare for it, I need to make sure I complete my morning routine and shield myself properly. I should also put a note on my desk as soon as I arrive at work to do my shielding exercises as soon as I feel negative energy, instead of absorbing it. Additionally, I need to remember that in life, not everyone is going to like me and that's okay.*

Hopefully, you've started making changes to your diet and incorporating exercise into your daily routine. If so, you will start noticing immediate changes. In Chapter 4, we will look at how negative energy affects highly sensitive people.

CHAPTER 4:

HOW NEGATIVE ENERGY AFFECTS HIGHLY SENSITIVE PEOPLE

Science proves that everything is made up of energy, and that energy is constantly vibrating. Experts refer to this as "the law of vibration." What most of us are unaware of is how that energy affects us, and, most importantly, the energy released from other people. As a highly sensitive person, you will have experienced gut instincts about people that you can't explain. As soon as you meet certain people, you either like them, or you don't. You were sensing their vibrational energy.

Energy attracts energy—you will find that positive people, haters, drama queens and complainers all associate with the same energy patterns. Pay attention to angry or depressed people; in general, you will find that they attract unpleasant circumstances, low-paying jobs, and negative people. Because of their vibration, they attract everything they don't want and become even more depressed and angry because nothing seems to go right. Their lives enter into a downward spiral that's difficult to recover from. On the other hand, grateful and happy people attract everything they want—and this doesn't necessarily mean material wealth. They exhibit an infectious joy because their vibrational energy is high. They are surrounded by the right people, and they seem to cruise through life.

Your mind is an energy field, and according to experts, we think at least 6000 thoughts per day. These thoughts create emotions that send out vibrational waves, flowing through every cell in your body before being sent out into the universe. Not only does the mind create powerful energetic vibrations—so does the heart. Author and business executive Howard Martin found that our hearts emit an even stronger electromagnetic field than our brains. I went to one of his talks during which he conducted an experiment with the audience. We were asked to sit next to a random person and send heart energy to each other. We were then told to turn away from that person and write down what we were sensing. Everyone in the room sensed the same thing as the person they had teamed up with! In other words, not only are we sending out vibrations; we are receiving them too.

This is why the law of attraction exists, the basic premise being that like attracts like. In other words, you will attract the same frequency you are vibrating at. Science works in the same way; two droplets of water will slowly move towards each other until they become one. They can't remain separate if the water droplets are in the same environment. But the same is not true of a droplet of oil and a droplet of water—no matter how close they get to each other, they won't become one because their vibrations are different.

What Does This Mean For HSPs?

The average person can sit in a room with a group of people who have negative energy and not get greatly affected by it—even if the individual has a positive mindset and feels slightly uncomfortable around the negative energy. If everyone is complaining and gossiping, the person with positive energy will either avoid joining in with the discussion, or will turn it into a more uplifting talk. They leave, go home, and forget about what's just taken place. Highly sensitive people don't have this luxury because we absorb energy. Negative energy will make the HSP feel depressed, anxious, judgmental, jealous, manipulative, greedy, hateful, sad, confused, and angry. It destroys your confidence and pushes you to self-destructive behaviors, which make you feel miserable all the time. Mental health issues can also occur when the depression and anxiety take such a strong hold on you that you can't overcome them. Negative energy can cause the following:

Confusion: People with negative energy will not only exhaust you, they will also confuse you.

Restlessness: Negative energy in the body shows up as tension. When your mind is overtaken by negative thoughts, you feel emotions such as sadness or anger. You will find it difficult to shake these feelings, which results in restlessness.

Chronic Pain: Negative energy causes tension and constriction in the muscles. When the body is under stress, it causes physical pain.

Anxiety/Depression: Negative energy alters your mood and can make you feel depressed and anxious.

Breathlessness: Energy expert and Reiki master Stacee Magee states that grief settles in the lungs. You may not have experienced grief directly, but if someone in your environment has, and they are sending out negative energy, you may find it difficult to breathe.

Stomachache: Another physical sign of negative energy in your physical environment or body is a stomachache. Sometimes your stomachache might not have anything to do with what you've eaten; it can be that the negative energy has caused tension in your stomach.

Headache: If you're not dehydrated or in an environment that's too noisy, a dull headache acts as a messenger that negative energy is surrounding you.

Adrenal Fatigue: Adrenal fatigue makes you feel overwhelmed, exhausted, and unable to think clearly. It can also cause you to crave carb-filled, salty, and sugary foods. Adrenal fatigue can make you put on weight and feel anxious.

How to Protect Yourself Against Negative Energy

I really wish I had a magic wand to zap negative energy out of the world, but I don't, and I'm sure you don't either, so the only thing you can do is protect yourself against it. The reality is that you're going to encounter negative energy all the time. Everyone can deal with their own negative energy. As long as we are aware that our vibrations are low, we can pretty much control our energy levels—but we can't control other people's. You might live at home with your parents, or in an apartment with your friends, and if they're carrying negative energy, there's not much you can do about it. When I lived at home with my parents, I was always sick and depressed, and I hated being in the house. I dreaded coming home from work every night—sometimes I'd sit in my car until I knew everyone was asleep before going inside. I didn't understand why until I learned about the effects of negative energy. Here are some of the tips I use to protect myself:

How to Open and Close Your Energy Field

The first lesson I learned when I started seeing an energy healer was that you can open and close your own energy field. It's like a door; you open it when you want to let people in, and you shut it when people leave. But not only do you shut it—you lock it so they can't come back in. Imagine if you just left your front door open all the time. You would have all types of undesirables walking in and out of your home. Energy is no different. When your energy field is constantly open, you may as well have a sign on your forehead saying, *"All energy types welcome."* When you learn to open and close your energy field, you will become more intuitive and alert when it's open, and more peaceful and relaxed when it's closed.

How to Open Your Energy Field

When you open your energy field, you are activating yourself to receive from the spiritual world. Here are the steps you need to take:

1. Have a purpose or intention for what you want to achieve.
2. Have an activation code.
3. Turn on your energy light.
4. Express gratitude.

Have a Purpose or Intention for What You Want to Achieve

As you have read, thoughts are energy. When setting your purpose or intention, it's all about what thoughts you are projecting into the atmosphere. Ask to channel to and connect with the other side and state the reason why. You can open your energy to help others, or yourself.

Have an Activation Code

An activation code is a personal prayer, energy imprint, signature, symbol, or saying. You can modify the words depending on the intention. Some people might like to visualize a symbol or cultivate a feeling (energy imprint) in their body beforehand. I prefer to say a prayer, but you can experiment and see what you are most comfortable with. Here is the prayer that I say:

> *"Intelligent, infinite Creator, thank you for choosing me to be a vessel to reach your people. I am forever grateful for your love. I am also grateful for the guides you've given me. Please connect me with them at this time to assist me on my assignment today. I am grateful for the protection, and I know that you have already given me what I've asked for.*
>
> *Thank you for all that you do."*

You can ask for anything that gives you access to your higher self and strengthens your connection to the spiritual realm. It's important that you're specific about what you want for yourself and for others because whatever you ask for is what you're going to get. Once your energy field has been opened, you might feel tingling in your hands as your energy makes its way through your body.

Switch on Your Energy Light

I find this part exciting! Visualize yourself as a light bulb that you have the power to turn off and on with a dimmer switch. Once your energy field is open, turn your light on. Imagine you are turning on each chakra from the bottom to the top, and gradually turn the dimmer switch up. As you turn on each chakra, imagine the most brilliant and bright colors. Once they are all turned on, shine your light outwards, and see it expanding from within your body, and then illuminating out of your body. Your entire body now radiates a brilliant light full of your powerful energy that expands out to other dimensions.

Express Gratitude

Now that you are ready to use your energy for the purpose or intention for which it was set, express gratitude to the Creator for allowing it to happen.

How to Close Your Energy Field

When you close your energy field, you are shutting yourself off from the spiritual world. It's important that you close your energy field immediately to ensure that nothing unwanted comes in when it's open. Here are the steps you need to take:

1. Set an intention to close your energy field.
2. Say a prayer of thanksgiving for closing your energy field.
3. Turn off the light.
4. Express gratitude that your energy field has been locked.

Set an Intention to Close your Energy Field

Now that your mission has been accomplished, you must set the intention to close your energy field.

Say a Prayer of Thanksgiving for Closing your Energy Field

Express gratitude to the Creator and to your guides for allowing you to open your energy field and access the spiritual world. Here is the deactivating prayer I say to close my energy field:

> "Intelligent, infinite Creator, and the guides who helped me open my energy field and access the spiritual realm. I thank you immensely for allowing me to help myself and others. I am now requesting that my energy field is closed.
>
> Thank you for all that you do."

Turn Off the Light

Visualize your chakras, and one by one close them by turning your dimmer switch all the way down. Start from your head, and make your way down your body. Keep your first and last chakra partway open so you are connected to the Divine and grounded with Earth. You may like to imagine that each chakra has a little door attached to it with a lock on it. This works for some people—but do whatever you're comfortable with. By turning off your lights and closing your energy field, you won't attract any unwanted energy.

Express Gratitude that Your Energy Field Has Been Locked

Now that you've closed your energy field, express gratitude to your Creator and guides for locking your energy field.

Once the session is over, eat or drink something light and healthy to ground yourself. It will stimulate your digestive system and give you the energy you need to go about your day.

How to Protect Yourself Against Negative People

As mentioned, we can't rid the world of negative energy, which means we can't rid the world of negative people; therefore, our only option is to protect ourselves from them. Here are some tips:

Ignore Them: People with negative energy operate in many fraudulent ways in an attempt to steal your energy. One tactic they use is to greet you with seemingly high positive energy and then flip the switch on you. They will smile widely and act as if they are overjoyed to see you, but once they are confident they have you in their territory, they unleash their negative energy onto you, and you end up feeling overwhelmed and suffocated. This is how it usually goes: A friend calls and asks if you want to go out for lunch, and you agree, thinking nothing of it. As soon as you both get comfortable, you've ordered coffee and exchanged pleasantries, she unleashes the dragon and begins telling you about all the problems she's currently having. The issue isn't that she's telling you her problems—it's that she didn't give you any advance warning that this was why you were having lunch. If that was the case, you could have prepared yourself for what was coming or declined the invitation.

My first piece of advice when it comes to meeting up with friends is to get confirmation about the type of meeting it is going to be. Ask what they are planning on speaking about. This sounds extreme, but if you don't ask, you'll never know, and you'll keep walking into situations that overwhelm you. Obviously, sometimes the conversation is going to go off track, but if it does and you find it distressing, it's up to you to either shut it down or leave.

Don't Look at the Person: When the X-Men character Scott Summers first discovered his superpower, it came in the form of uncontrollable energy anytime he experienced intense emotions. This intense energy shot out from his eyes and destroyed everything he came into contact with. Until Summers learned how to control his energy, he caused himself and others a lot of damage. It is a scientific fact that energy is transmitted through the eyes, and, like Scott Summers, unless you know how to control your energy, you are going to destroy everything you look at. This is why it's important not to look people who have negative energy in the eyes—because they will send it right to you. When you find yourself standing face to face with a person who has negative energy, look at their nose, mouth or forehead—but not the eyes— and end the interaction as quickly as possible.

Get Out of Their Space: I had a terrible experience a few years back where my mother had to stay with me for over a year after having a stroke. In the beginning, we would eat at the dining table together every evening, and I would go back to my room feeling totally demoralized and drained. I would eat my meal as quickly as possible just to get away from the table. Every night, the same scene would play out: She would scream at me for eating too fast, and then spend the rest of the time either insulting other people or just moaning in general. I was constantly trying to direct the conversation in a positive direction because my ears couldn't stand to hear her vile talk. Finally, I had to make the decision to eat in my bedroom so we were not in the same space for too long. If she was in the kitchen and I needed to get something to eat, I'd wait until she had left before I went in. Basically, I made sure we were never in the same room together.

If you start feeling off when certain people are around—be it people you live with (family, roommates) or the general public—*move*. Depending on the size of the room, try to enforce a minimum distance of 20 feet between you and the offending party. Forget about not wanting to upset anyone—this is about preserving your mental health and well-being. If the energy vampire (someone who drains your energy) sits next to you, move, to avoid absorbing their negative energy.

How to Raise Your Vibrations

When you're vibrating on a high frequency, it's difficult for negative energy to attach itself to you. I have cultivated a habit of raising my vibrations daily, and topping up when I'm about to enter an environment where negative energy might be lingering. There are several ways you can raise your vibrations. Here is what works best for me:

Your Soul Light: One way of raising your vibration is to shine your soul light. There will be times when you are unable to open and close your energy fully. Life is unpredictable, and you can end up in unexpected situations. When this happens, you leave yourself open to negative energy. It can be so overpowering that you may not know where it's coming from. When this happens, you can shine your soul light to raise your vibration, and the person or people with negative energy will become so uncomfortable, they'll leave.

How to Shine Your Soul Light

- Take a deep breath in and release all the air by breathing out slowly.

- Breathe in and breathe out again, letting go of all expectations and worries.

- Take a deep breath in and release all the air by breathing out slowly one last time.

- Visualize your heart chakra (your chest) with a bright light in it.

- Imagine that your heart chakra is slowly growing bigger and bigger.

- Visualize a golden, pink, or green color. Once your chakra is fully grown, imagine it opening and a brilliant light shining from your chest.

- This light illuminates your entire being and expands beyond your body.

- Imagine that you've become a part of the universe.

To better understand how this works, think about an extremely powerful flashlight shining through your body. That's your soul light. It belongs to you. If you are finding the process difficult, call on your guides to help you. Once you've raised your vibrations, and the negative energy has left your environment, switch off your soul light.

Meditation: You can meditate in several ways, but the most basic form is vipassana. This is also referred to as breathing meditation, and it's perfect for beginners. Studies prove that meditation has several benefits. One such benefit is that it improves gray matter in the brain, which makes us more relaxed and focused. It also helps to raise your vibrations and helps you develop a deeper body-mind connection. Experts state that meditating for as little as 10 minutes per day has significant benefits. If you are a beginner, you will likely find that your thoughts and feelings are all over the place. Don't worry about it—the more you practice, the better you will become. It's actually very common, and in meditation circles, it's referred to as "monkey mind." Here is a meditation routine I use every day:

- Sit in a comfortable position with your back straight and your legs crossed. Position your right hand on top of your left hand and place your hands in your lap.

- Close your eyes and begin taking deep breaths. Inhale through your nose, and exhale through your mouth.

- Focus on the sound of your breath and how it feels when it enters your nostrils and travels into your lungs. Your diaphragm should be moving.

- Your thoughts and emotions will distract you. Bring your mind back to your breath when it wanders.

Meditation isn't only about focusing on your breath. You can also focus on an object, or on sounds. For example, if you are meditating outside, you can focus on a leaf, or on the sound of the wind. You can also play relaxing music while you meditate.

Repeat Mantras: Make mantras a part of your daily routine. They are an effortless way to generate positive energy and raise your vibrations. Mantras don't need to be complicated or long—spend a few minutes a day meditating on them, or repeat them as you go about your day. They will keep you focused on positive thoughts, and research suggests that mantras rewire the brain by reprogramming the subconscious mind. This is called autosuggestion and it involves constantly telling ourselves we are successful and happy until we start to believe it. Here are a few of my favorite mantras:

- *"I am grateful for my life."*
- *"Good things always happen to me."*
- *"I am a lover of life."*
- *"I live an abundant life."*
- *"I am healthy."*
- *"I am happy."*

The People You Associate With: I will discuss this further in Chapter 6. However, as you have read, vibrations also come from external sources. To keep your vibrations high, you need to associate with people who match them. Spend time with positive, happy people who are loving, supportive, and open-minded. The quality of your life will significantly improve once you start associating with the right people. Pettiness, gossip, and drama come from a place of negative vibrations and low consciousness. Stay away from such people.

Listen to Music: Music has a powerful impact on our state of consciousness and our emotions. What you allow into your ears influences your character and the frequency you vibrate on. As a highly sensitive person, it's best to listen to music that inspires, uplifts, and motivates you. The solfeggio scale is an ancient spiritual approach to music, used in sacred music such as the Gregorian chants. Science proves that it heals DNA, boosts energy levels, and improves well-being and happiness. There are six solfeggio frequencies, and they all have a specific benefit:

- **852hz:** Restores your spiritual foundation
- **741hz:** Improves your ability to express yourself
- **639hz:** Improves your relationships
- **528hz:** Heals your DNA
- **417hz:** Leads to positive life changes
- **396hz:** Frees you from fear and guilt

Practice Gratitude: In its simplest form, gratitude means being thankful for the good things in your life, from the smallest to the biggest things. All successful people, thought leaders, and spiritual masters are advocates of gratitude. They believe it's one of the requirements for true happiness. If we can't appreciate what we already have, we will never appreciate who we are about to become. Gratitude raises your vibrations because it gets you to focus on what you *do* have instead of on what you *don't* have. As highly sensitive people, it is easy to get depressed—all it takes is for us to turn on the TV, read a newspaper, or listen to the radio to put us in a place of despair. Once we are there, we can find it difficult to get out. But gratitude is one way to pull yourself out of a slump. I believe in gratitude because it works for me. I also believe it should become a part of your daily routine. Here are five gratitude practices that you can incorporate into your life each day:

1. **Advance Gratitude:** I believe that all the good and bad things that are going to happen in your life have already been established in the spirit realm. Whatever manifests depends on the energy you give it. The idea is to give thanks for what you want before you get it. For example, if you've got a presentation coming up, give thanks for how well it's going to go. This is a powerful form of gratitude because you've already tuned into the energy of success before the day arrives. By putting the right energy into the atmosphere, the universe will follow through. It strengthens your faith, deepens your connection with the Divine, and improves your mental state.

2. **Be Grateful During Bad Times:** *"What?"* I can hear you saying. Okay, let me explain. True happiness is about being content in both good and bad situations. If there's one thing we know for sure, it's that adversity is going to knock on everyone's door at some point in life. We can't escape from it—it's as certain as death. If your happiness is dependent upon your circumstances, happiness will have fun playing hide-and-seek with you throughout your life. No one likes pain, but if you pay attention, you will find a lesson in the blessing. Additionally, being grateful during bad times isn't about being thankful for the situation you've found yourself in; it's about continuing to keep your eyes fixed on the things you're grateful for. Life will always work itself out, no matter how bad it seems in the moment. So, when you're going through hell, keep your mind fixed on all the positive aspects of your life, and this will keep your vibrations up.

3. **Go on a Gratitude Walk:** Anytime you feel muddled and confused, go on a gratitude walk. While you are walking, pay attention to the things around you and point out the good in them. Notice a child's happy and innocent grin, the breeze against your face, the cute dog playing with its owner. The effort you make to step outside of yourself and focus on the good around you will cause you to see the beauty of the universe we live in. The walk will help you empty your mind and crystalize your thoughts so you can go home and face the situation that was agitating you.

4. **Keep a Gratitude Journal:** This is the most common form of gratitude because so many people have testified to its effectiveness. All you need is a small notepad and a pen. Every morning before you get out of bed, write out five things you are grateful for. Focus on them and the feeling of gratitude for five minutes. This morning practice will ensure you start your day off with high vibrations. Do the same thing before you go to sleep at night, and it will ensure you go to bed with high vibrations and an attitude of thankfulness. I haven't had a bad night's sleep since I started this practice.

5. **Create a Gratitude Jar:** All you need is a jar, shreds of paper big enough to write a sentence on, and a pen. It's similar to keeping a gratitude journal, but this involves writing down one thing you are grateful for every day, meditating on it, and putting it in the jar. When I'm feeling miserable, I go through the jar and reflect on the things I'm grateful for.

Be Present: Most people are unaware that their vibrations are low because they don't focus on the present. Their minds are all over the place thinking about everything other than what they're doing in that moment. In this present moment, the only thing you are doing is reading this book. But every so often, a thought or emotion will distract you and take your attention away from reading. Being present is similar to meditation; it's about bringing your awareness back to what you're doing and keeping it there for as long as possible. As you are reading, focus on your senses—what you can see, hear, and feel. Thoughts and emotions are going to distract you, but think of them as waves of consciousness. They come and they go. When you feel or think about something that makes you uncomfortable, don't try and fight it by reacting to it—instead, acknowledge that it's there and allow it to pass. Resistance causes hindrance. You will notice massive changes in your life when you stop resisting your thoughts and feelings and allow them to *be*.

Develop a Spiritual Routine: Protecting your energy as an HSP should become as normal as brushing your teeth in the morning. One of the reasons I was always so stressed out was because I went to bed late, woke up late, rushed to get ready and grabbed a McDonald's breakfast on the way to work. I was always frazzled and disheveled, and I drank endless cups of coffee so I could stay awake and focus, which just made me anxious and fidgety. My life was just one big mess, and I didn't know how to get it under control. But things radically changed once I developed a spiritual routine. I started going to bed at the same time every evening and waking up at the same time each morning. I woke up at 6:00 a.m., which gave me enough time to complete my routine, have breakfast, and get to work on time.

Today, my morning routine looks like this:

- Wake up at 6:00 a.m.
- Gratitude journal
- Go for a run
- Meditate
- Listen to something inspirational while getting ready

My evening routine looks like this:

- Saltwater-cleanse shower
- Visualize
- Gratitude journal
- Go to sleep listening to 417hz healing music

Your life is your responsibility. You can decide whether you want to own your personal power or not. Unfortunately, some people can be disrespectful and inconsiderate when it comes to your needs. In my experience, I've found that this is especially true of family members. My mother and older sister were the main culprits, and I have happily cut them out of my life with no regrets. If people are going to keep violating your space and your boundaries, you've got to put your foot down, no matter who they are. If not, you'll end up a very miserable and depressed person, blaming everyone else for your misfortune, despite the fact that you keep letting them into your life.

I get it—highly sensitive people find it difficult to enforce boundaries because they don't like conflict. But what's the tradeoff? Depletion and overwhelm or peace of mind? It took an extreme situation for me to decide that enough was enough. But you can put a stop to people with negative energy invading your space today if you are serious about tapping into your highest potential as a highly sensitive person.

FOODS THAT PROTECT AGAINST NEGATIVE ENERGY

Ancient Indian, African, and Chinese cultures have used various foods to protect themselves against negative energy since the beginning of time. I have tried just about every strategy ever written to shield myself, and I have found that some foods work extremely well:

Green Lemons: Lemons are also known as "the fruit of good." The principles of Vastu Shastra state that you can use lemons to detoxify your space and cleanse negative energy in the following ways:

- The citrus fragrance helps improve mood and cleanse the atmosphere.

- Lemons restore positive energy after trauma, the loss of a loved one, or after attending a funeral.

- They cleanse the mind and body of nervous tension, depression, and anxiety.

How to Use Lemons

- Place three green lemons at the door of your home. You will know they've absorbed negative energy because they'll start turning black or yellow. Once the color starts changing, throw them away and replace them.

- Keep three lemons in your desk draw at work, or your purse. This will help eliminate the negative energy associated with hatred, jealousy, and envy, and will keep you balanced.

- Add lemon juice to water combined with bicarbonate of soda to remove the stickiness and spray it around your home, especially in the corners.

- Collect rainwater and use it to boil lemon skins, allowing the fragrance to flow around your home.

- Squeeze lemon juice into water and use a cloth to rub it onto your jewelry. This cleansing process will remove negative energy from the items and protect you against it when you are out and about.

- Put three lemons in a bowl and keep them by your bedside table. This will protect you from any negative energy sent to you in your sleep. Again, when they start turning black or yellow, throw them away and replace them.

- Arrange four lemons in the shape of a cross, sprinkle salt around them in the shape of a circle, and then put it under your bed before you sleep. The next morning, tip the lemons into a plastic bag without touching them and throw them in the trash outside your home. Do this until you feel the negative energy has left you. It should take around three days. This will protect you against the negative energy you have absorbed throughout the day.

- Slice a lemon into four slices and sprinkle salt on each slice. Place the lemon at the entrance of your home, and it will absorb the negative energy of anyone who approaches your door. Repeat this for three days in a row for the best results.

Salt and Water: Salt and water are powerful energetic cleansers, making the perfect combination for several reasons. Science proves that water holds on to the vibrations and emotions that have been emitted intentionally or unintentionally from the things or people it's surrounded by. You can use this to your advantage when it comes to cleansing your energy.

Salt assists in the cleansing process because it can be used to transform or transmute inharmonious and dense energies into positive, harmless energy. For this reason, salt has been used as a cleansing agent as far back as the sixteenth century when Roman Catholics used it to get rid of demonic forces.

How to Use Salt and Water: There are three ways you can use the saltwater cleansing method. To begin, you will need the following supplies:

- A bucket, bowl, shower, or bathtub
- Salt
- Water

I strongly recommend using Celtic sea salt, or Pink Himalayan salt, also known as rock salt. You can use regular table salt, but it's not as effective. These natural salts haven't been stripped or processed, so they still contain their naturally occurring trace elements and minerals. Table salt has been reduced to almost 100% sodium chloride, and what is more, it might have been bleached, or contain anti-caking agents or aluminum.

Have a Bath: Add one cup of salt to the bathtub and fill it with water. Stir the water with your hands to dissolve the salt. While you are filling the bath and stirring the water, set your intentions for the removal of negative energy. Soak in the bath for 30 minutes and then rinse the salt off in the shower. When you drain the water from the bath, imagine the negative energy flowing down the drain.

Use the Reiki technique mentioned earlier to wipe off any remnants of negative energy by gliding your hands over your aura and setting the intention that you are sweeping away the remaining negative energy. When you get down to your feet, use a flicking motion with your hands to send the negative energy down the drain.

Have a Shower: I personally don't like taking baths—I'm an action person and like to get things done quickly, and the whole process of filling up the bath just takes too long for me. So, my preferred method for a saltwater cleanse is to have a shower.

Set your intention before getting into the shower, and then sprinkle the salt into your washcloth. Rub the salty washcloth over your body before washing with soap. Add additional salt if you need to. When you rinse off, imagine the negative energy sliding off your body. You can also run your Reiki hands over your aura in the same way as when taking a bath.

Use a Bowl: Add salt and water to a bowl and set your intention. Dip your hands into the bowl and wipe your body down with your hands. You can use the Reiki method at the same time. Afterwards, wash your hands and imagine the negative energy being washed off and going down the drain.

Cinnamon: Cinnamon is the perfect cleansing agent because it's warm and spicy, and that is just how you want to feel. To perform this ritual, you will also need a crystal. I have used many crystals over the years, and I find the Manipura chakra crystals the most powerful. You can use standard clear quartz, sunstone, or citrine. In addition, you will need the following:

- Pen
- Paper
- Candle
- Crystal
- Cinnamon stick
- Candle holder

How to Use Cinnamon

Write down on a piece of paper the negative energy you want to release. Fold the paper up and place it in front of you.

Light the candle, and then light the cinnamon stick. Once it starts smoking, use it to trace the outline of your body, starting from your head. You may need to light the stick more than once to complete the process.

Rest the incense stick in a candle holder next to the burning candle. You can either stare at the flame of the candle or close your eyes. Slow your mind down by taking three deep breaths. Deeply inhale into your stomach and then out through your mouth. Visualize yourself releasing the negative energy, and notice the feelings of freedom once it has left you. Imagine that smoke is rising from your body in the form of a black cloud, going up into the air, through the earth's core and out into space where it disappears. Keep visualizing this until it feels real.

The final step is to burn the piece of paper.

Mustard Seeds and Salt: Indians have always placed a pot of mustard seeds in their homes for protection against evil spirits.

The practice is not just superstition—there is scientific evidence to back it up. Research suggests that one mustard seed generates a bioenergy field 100 times its radius. They activate the biochemical processes in the human body that promote healing. For this reason, there are many companies who sell mustard-seed mats. Mustard seeds are known to:

- Cure impotence and insomnia
- Relieve depression and anxiety
- Relieve migraines
- Soothe muscle aches and joint pain
- Eliminate back pain

How to Use Mustard Seeds and Salt

It is easier to perform this ritual with someone else, but you can also do it alone. Use organic mustard seeds and Celtic or Himalayan pink salt.

- In a small bowl, combine one handful of salt and another of mustard seeds.

- Start by setting your intentions for the removal of the negative energy you've absorbed.

- Sit on a low chair facing east and bend your knees up towards your chest.

- Pick up some salt and mustard seeds in both hands and make closed fists.

- Cross your arms over the front of your body.

- Uncross your arms and, in a clockwise direction, move the right fist from your head to your feet.

- In an anticlockwise direction, trace your left fist over your body from head to foot.

- Touch the ground with both fists and start again.

- At the end, put the mustard seeds and salt into a plastic bag and throw them in the trash outside your home.

Bay Leaf: Bay leaf is also known as "bay laurel." This powerful herb is a favorite amongst energy healers. It is useful for psychic development, cleansing, protection, prosperity, and manifestation. You can either grow it in your home or garden, or purchase some from an herbalist.

Burning bay leaf will drive out and cleanse any harmful and unwanted negative energies and feelings that other people have brought into your space. Bay leaf also works well with sage when performing a sacred cleansing.

How to Use Bay Leaf: You can do this at any time, but you will get the most benefit from it during a full moon. Take some bay leaves and write all your fears, worries, and anxieties on them. Spend time focusing on these unwanted feelings, letting all your stress flow out of your system into the bay leaf. Once you feel relief, burn the bay leaf while watching the smoke transform your worries into positive energy and carry it out into the universe.

Emotional overload is crippling for highly sensitive people, and if you are going to operate within your full potential, learning how to deal with it is important. Keep reading to find out how to beat emotional overload.

CHAPTER 5:

HOW TO BEAT EMOTIONAL OVERLOAD

Whether you've had a disagreement with your partner or been cut off on the road, as a highly sensitive person, it's easy to become overwhelmed. To make matters worse, we also experience the emotions of others, which intensifies our emotional overload. I remember an incident that happened at my last job. I noticed one of my colleagues leaving the office in a hurry just before lunchtime. I could sense that something was wrong, so I followed her. By the time she stepped outside, she was in tears, and I asked her if she was okay. She didn't want to talk near the building, so we sat in my car and she explained what had happened. The further Janet got into the story, the angrier I became. She was extremely upset, and so was I—she had been treated very unfairly. I was so enraged that I wanted to go and give the perpetrators a piece of my mind. Janet and I stayed in the car talking, and I listened. She didn't want to do anything about it; she just wanted to release her frustration.

By the time we got back to the office, Janet was calm, levelheaded and ready to get back to work. She sat at her desk, talking and laughing with the colleagues who had upset her, and she was fine. Meanwhile, I was sitting at my desk burning with anger, shaking, palms sweating and almost in tears because I couldn't believe how rude these people were, and I wanted to tell them exactly how I felt. I was completely exhausted, and I just wanted the day to end so I could go home and curl up in bed. The problem was that it wasn't my fight. Janet was fine, laughing and smiling—while I was now carrying her burden.

It wasn't Janet's fault; I was the one who encouraged her to speak to me about what had happened. Highly sensitive people have a deep desire to make the world a better place, but there are some things we just can't handle because we are like sponges, absorbing everything. It's tempting to stop being so compassionate, but that's not in our nature—however, we do need to protect ourselves against emotional overload. Here are some tips on how to do this:

Manage Your Emotions

Although emotions play an important role in our daily lives, when they are out of control they can become destructive and have a negative effect on our overall well-being and interpersonal relationships. Therapist Vicki Botnick states that even the emotions we view as positive, such as joy and elation, can get so intense that they are difficult to control. However, with a bit of work, you can learn to manage your emotions so they don't overwhelm you. Here are some tips:

Pay Attention to the Impact of Your Emotions

There is nothing wrong with having intense emotions—they make our lives vibrant, exciting, and unique. Strong feelings are a sign that we are fully embracing life and not stifling our natural reactions. It's also normal to feel overwhelmed sometimes, like when something really amazing or tragic happens. But how do you know when your emotions are out of control? Emotions that are out of control will cause:

- Emotional or physical outbursts
- An urge to control our emotions through substance abuse
- Difficulty at school or work
- Problems relating to others
- Conflict in friendships or relationships

Take some time out to evaluate how your uncontrolled emotions are affecting your day-to-day life.

REGULATE YOUR EMOTIONS—DON'T REPRESS THEM

Highly sensitive people are experts at repressing their emotions. For most of us, we learn to do this at a young age because we were raised in households where our high sensitivity wasn't understood. Additionally, because we feel emotions so deeply, we find them difficult to control. Unfortunately, we can't control them with a dial—it would be great if it was that easy! But you can *imagine* that you have that ability. You wouldn't want to have your emotions turned up to the highest level all the time, nor would you want them turned down to the lowest level. When you suppress your emotions, you put a restriction on expressing your feelings. This can happen on a conscious or a subconscious level. Whichever way your emotions are suppressed, it can cause physical and mental health problems such as:

- Muscle pain and tension
- Substance abuse
- Inability to manage stress

- Sleep problems
- Depression
- Anxiety

Controlling your emotions is not about brushing them under the carpet. Healthy emotional expression is about finding the right balance between no emotion and overwhelming emotions.

LABEL YOUR FEELINGS

Paying attention to your mood can help you gain control of your emotions. Let's say you've just started dating someone, and you tried arranging another date with them, but they didn't have time. Two days ago, you tried texting, asking if you could meet up, and you've just received a reply saying, *"Unavailable this weekend."* As soon as you open the message, you get really upset. You don't take a step back and process the information—you just throw the phone against the wall, kick over your laundry basket and sprawl out on the bed in floods of tears. The next time something like this happens, stop and ask yourself the following questions:

- **How do I feel right now?** *(Angry, confused, disappointed)*
- **What triggered this feeling?** *(I thought the way he responded was rude.)*
- **Is there another explanation that is more reasonable?** *(Maybe he's going through something he doesn't feel like explaining to me.)*
- **How do I want to express these feelings?** *(Cry, scream, smash my phone)*
- **Is there a better way I can cope with these feelings?** *(Ask if he's feeling okay, go for a run, take a forest bath)*

By thinking about the alternatives to your situation, you are reframing your thoughts, which can help you express your emotions in a way that doesn't cause you or anyone else harm. It will take a while before this way of responding to difficult situations becomes a habit, but keep practicing—it will get easier over time.

Accept All of Your Emotions

I found that when I started working on controlling my emotions, I would try and convince myself that things weren't really that bad. When you get so excited that you can't breathe because your sister has just announced she's pregnant again, or when you start crying uncontrollably because your neighbor's cat just died, you might think that telling yourself to calm down or to stop overreacting will help. But in doing so, you're telling yourself that your feelings aren't that important—and isn't this what you've been fighting against your entire life? Your feelings are valid, and they matter to you because that's how you feel. Accepting your emotions as you feel them will train you to become comfortable with them. Getting comfortable with intense emotions allows you to completely accept them without having an extreme reaction that won't help you.

Start viewing your emotions as messengers. They are neutral, neither good nor bad—and even if they don't *feel* good, they want to communicate something important to you. For example, if you keep getting upset because you're always losing your work log-in card, maybe it's a message that you need to get something to attach it to and hang it around your neck. Accepting your emotions in this way can lead to greater satisfaction and fewer mental health problems. Additionally, if you can think of your emotions as helpful, you will lead a happier and more fulfilling life.

Keep an Emotions Journal: Writing down how you feel and the reactions you have can help you pinpoint disruptive patterns. Getting your feelings out of your head and onto the page will allow you to reflect on them at a deeper level. It will also give you insight into specific circumstances such as family conflict, or problems at work that play a role in the emotions you find difficult to control. When you understand what triggers you, it makes finding ways to manage your emotions easier. You will get the most benefit out of journaling if you do it every day. Take your journal with you when you leave the house, and record any intense feelings or emotions as they happen. Write down what triggered the emotion and how you reacted to it. If your reaction was unhelpful, write down reactions that could have been more beneficial, for future reference.

Deep Breathing: Deep breathing is discussed in more detail in Chapter 8. In addition to helping with stress, it is also useful for managing your emotions when you are in a state of euphoria, or extremely angry. Deep breathing won't eliminate the emotion (remember, that's not the aim), but it will help you ground yourself so you can step back and evaluate your emotions. The next time you feel your emotions spinning out of control, do this breathing exercise:

- Take a slow, deep breath in from your diaphragm.
- Once your lungs are full, hold your breath and count to three.
- Exhale slowly, releasing all the breath from your lungs.
- You can add to the breathing exercise by repeating a mantra like, "I am relaxed," or "I am calm."

Express Yourself at the Right Time: Sometimes it's inappropriate to display intense emotions. As the saying goes, "There's a time and a place for everything." Even though you're a highly sensitive person and you feel emotions more intensely than others, it's important that you don't express them at the wrong time. Please don't misinterpret what I'm saying and assume I'm asking you to suppress your emotions or hide the fact that you're highly sensitive. I know from personal experience that sometimes we feel that people are being insensitive towards us when we express our emotions. What I've found, however, is that it's generally not because they're being insensitive, but because my emotions were released at the wrong time. I remember being at a boyfriend's dinner party. They were serving chicken, and I started feeling sick and upset because I was thinking about the pain the chicken must have gone through for it to be on the dinner table. One of his friends blurted out, "This chicken is absolutely delicious!" I completely lost it, screaming about how the chicken had been slaughtered and had suffered just so that selfish humans could eat it. The entire table went quiet. I sat there red-faced, and my boyfriend was totally embarrassed. Needless to say, I was dumped that same evening.

On the other hand, your work colleagues would understand if you collapsed in a heap on the floor because you were just told that your mother had died. Being mindful of the situation and your surroundings will give you an idea as to whether it's okay to release your feelings in that moment.

Step Back From the Situation: Giving yourself space from the situation and separating yourself from intense feelings will give you the chance to evaluate your emotions and determine whether your response is reasonable. You can either physically remove yourself from the situation or you can do so mentally by distracting yourself. Again, let me be clear: by distracting yourself, I'm not telling you to ignore how you're feeling—the distraction is temporary so you can deal with your emotions when the time is right. To distract yourself, try:

- Talking to a friend
- Playing with your pet
- Watching a comedy
- Taking a walk

Meditation: Meditation helps to increase awareness of your experiences and feelings. The practice trains you to sit with your feelings; to acknowledge them without trying to get rid of them or judging yourself. As mentioned, when you accept all your emotions, it makes it easier for you to regulate them. Meditation helps you to sharpen those acceptance skills.

Stress Management: Managing your emotions is a lot more difficult when you're under a lot of stress. As stated in Chapter 3, stress is a normal part of life, and we can't escape from it. However, intense stress should not be a normal part of your life—and by practicing the tips provided in Chapter 3, you will be able to manage your emotions more effectively.

Talk to a Therapist: If you continue struggling with your emotions, you might need to see a therapist. Long-term, persistent mood swings and dysregulation are linked to mental health conditions such as bipolar disorder and borderline personality disorder. They can also be related to family issues, trauma, and other underlying concerns. A therapist can provide judgment-free, compassionate support as you:

- Practice reframing and challenging feelings that upset you
- Learn how to manage your emotions
- Get a better understanding of your mood swings
- Challenge the reasons why you find it difficult to manage your emotions.

Intense emotions and mood swings can elicit feelings of despair and hopelessness. This destructive cycle can lead to unhelpful coping methods such as self-harm or suicidal thoughts. If you ever start thinking about self-harm or suicide, it's important that you speak to someone you trust so they can help you get the support you need.

As loving and as accepting as highly sensitive people are, we can't let everyone into our lives, and for the sake of your mental health, you've got to be ruthless about keeping the wrong people out of it. In Chapter 6, we will explore this further.

CHAPTER 6:

LETTING PEOPLE INTO YOUR HIGHLY SENSITIVE WORLD

As I mentioned earlier, after my mother had a stroke, we lived under the same roof for over a year, and I was chronically depressed the whole time. She has terrible energy and is extremely untidy. As much as I tried to clean up, my apartment was what I considered unlivable for an entire year. I moved into the spare room and my mother took the biggest room. I organized my belongings as best as I could, but it was never good enough. Before my mom's arrival, my apartment was set up in a way that accommodated my highly sensitive nature. Everything was disrupted when she arrived, and it was the most difficult season of my life. I just about survived it, but for the sake of my mental health, I will never allow someone into my space like that again, family or not.

RELATIONSHIPS THAT ARE NOT GOOD FOR HSP

My closest friend during high school (we will call her Sandra) was a crazymaker. According to Julia Cameron, author of *The Artist's Way*, crazymakers are personalities that are always surrounded by controversy. They are charismatic and charming—

but for an HSP they are a whirlwind of destruction. Sandra and I had an extremely toxic friendship. I was the child, and she was the parent. I did what she told me to do and copied everything she did. I hung on to her every word as she re-enacted her dramatic adventures. At that time, I didn't have any boundaries, and I let her get way too close. Everything about her life affected me. Her demands were completely irrational, but when she told me to jump, my response was, "How high?"

The few times I said "No," she got really angry, so I quickly learned to do as I was told. It wasn't until we went off to different colleges and there was enough distance between us that I felt safe enough to sever the relationship. As a highly sensitive person, I've always found it difficult to make and keep friends, which is one of the main reasons I held on to such a toxic friendship for so many years. Additionally, society tells us that we need a large group of close friends in order to be complete. But the reality is that there are some friendships you should avoid, especially as a highly sensitive person.

What do HSPs Need From Their Friends?

Friendships are about quality, not quantity. There have been times in my life when I've only had one close friend and felt totally content because they were the perfect match for my unique needs. For HSPs, the ideal friendship is a meaningful one; we thrive on deep, solid, and strong connections. You can compare our friendships to the Wi-Fi signal on a phone. We are always looking for a friendship signal, but if that signal is weak, so is the connection. Having a deep connection with someone means feeling safe during our most vulnerable moments, knowing that someone hears us when they listen, and that the depth we share is reciprocated. I have spoken to many highly sensitive people about their needs in a friendship, mainly because I wanted to know if how I was feeling was normal. I found that this is what we need in order to have meaningful friendships. Shallow friendships are draining, and when we hold on to them, they can have a disastrous impact on our mental and emotional well-being. We are often made to feel as if we are being overly picky about life, and this includes our friendships. But it's important to remember that we have the right to be happy just as everyone else does, and if that means you're selective about your friends, then so be it. Here are a few types of friendships you should make a conscious decision to stay away from:

Judgmental Friendships: You should be able to own your high sensitivity with pride. Unfortunately, this is impossible when the people closest to you are constantly putting you down. We need our loved ones to be accepting and supportive of who we are. This is especially important if you've just discovered that you're highly sensitive and need to be surrounded by people who will lovingly guide you on your journey. A judgmental friend will directly or indirectly let you know that you are somehow abnormal for being highly sensitive. They will mock your choices by laughing at you or telling you that you need to get over it. They also have a tendency to show annoyance and impatience anytime you start feeling anxious in a social situation or need extra time to process information. You will feel nervous and uncomfortable around a friend like this. They will restrict your wings and prevent you from flying.

The Demanding Friendship: The type of person who calls you if you don't respond to a message five minutes after it was sent. They call you at all hours, even at night, just because they can't sleep and feel like talking. If you don't answer, they'll blow your phone up until you wake up! Once they've got you on the phone, you're not going back to sleep until they're done with the conversation.

Highly sensitive people need space to recharge—whether you're an introvert or an extrovert, you need time alone to process things and avoid overstimulation. You find it difficult to bounce from one event to the next. But some people don't understand this need and won't give you any space. They will demand that you stay at the club until it closes, and if you need to leave early or don't show up at all, they'll chastise you for it. Highly sensitive people find demanding behavior very stressful. You are often given an ultimatum that will harm you no matter what you choose. Let your friend down, or deal with the burnout or overwhelm that will overtake you when you socialize in the wrong environment. After a while, you'll start feeling resentful, and there's a high chance you'll have an emotional outburst later down the line.

Draining Friendships: Highly sensitive people are extremely compassionate and empathetic. They are often the go-to people when someone needs to talk about their problems. HSPs attract individuals who need someone to listen to them. Having this gift isn't the problem—the world needs it; however, HSPs attract people who take advantage of them. They become the sounding boards for everyone else, but it's not reciprocated. When the highly sensitive person needs someone to talk to, there's no one in sight.

While helping each other and sharing burdens is an essential part of a good friendship, HSPs need boundaries to avoid feeling drained. As you are aware, highly sensitive people absorb emotions, which means anytime a friend wants to discuss their problems, those emotions are felt deeply by the HSP. To prevent this, highly sensitive people need friends who respect their energy, the kind who won't take too much and become a burden.

Shallow Friendships: Highly sensitive people don't enjoy small talk, but it's easy to get trapped in friendships of this nature. It used to happen to me all the time and I'd end up having to block people. Whether at a work do or a social gathering, some individuals feel the need to collect as many contact details as possible and will ask for your phone number when your conversation is drawing to a close. You'll never hear from many of these people again, but there are some who will call you, with nothing of substance to talk about. They gossip, talk about the latest reality TV show or what's going on in the lives of their favorite celebrities. Highly sensitive people can't stomach these conversations because the highly sensitive mind needs something deep and meaningful for stimulation.

Don't Feel Guilty About Leaving Toxic Friendships

I used to hate ending friendships—it made me feel terrible. But at the same time, I literally felt as if a weight had been lifted off my shoulders when I did. As a highly sensitive person, self-care is so important; without it, we wouldn't survive in this chaotic world. Once you know what you need in order to thrive as an HSP, you are the only person responsible for ensuring you get those things. I'm sure many of you reading this can relate; you make a commitment to a toxic friend and spend the rest of the week complaining to yourself about it. Your journey to meet your friend is spent muttering under your breath about how inconvenient this is. When you get there, you feel uncomfortable and wish you hadn't come. On the way home, you are overwhelmed and exhausted, blaming everyone for how you feel apart from yourself.

As far as I'm concerned, one of the most important aspects of self-care is maintaining healthy relationships. If you absorb negative energy, it makes absolutely zero sense to associate with people who are constantly transmitting negative energy. Eventually, it will destroy you.

I am a firm believer in divine alignment—in other words, there are people you are destined to connect with. But I also believe you can block these connections by associating with people who are not a part of your destiny. You were meant to meet them for one reason only: so you know who not to invite into your life. In saying that, there is no social rule that says you must tolerate toxic people, even if they are friends or family members. You can't sacrifice your happiness for the sake of others. It's also important to mention that cutting off a friendship isn't always permanent. One of my closest friends today is someone I had to sever ties with after college because she was so toxic. But she completely changed a couple of years later; her mom died and the experience put life in perspective for her. Today, she's one of the kindest, most considerate people I know. We needed that time apart because we weren't good for each other at that particular moment in our lives, but now we have the perfect friendship.

How to End a Toxic Friendship

I don't agree with just blocking people. I have been guilty of this in the past, and it makes things very awkward when you bump into them again. This has happened to me more times than I care to remember. The best way to end a toxic friendship is by being honest. Start by telling your friend why their behavior is having a negative effect on you. If they don't listen, let them know you'll be abandoning the friendship. It's like the film *Mean Girls,* where Tina Fey tells her girlfriends they should stop calling each other sluts and whores because it gives men the green light to do the same. The moral of the story is that people will only treat you the way you allow them to treat you. Therefore, it's important to stand up for yourself and dictate how you want to be treated. Here are some tips on how to end a toxic friendship:

Acceptance: The first step in ending the friendship is admitting that the relationship is toxic. You know it's toxic because of the way it makes you feel. To be certain you are making the right decision, consider the following points:

- How is the relationship benefiting you? Do you feel miserable and depressed after spending time with them? Do you have fun when you're together?

- Accept you can't change them: I am always willing to give second chances to people who are prepared to change, but if they're not, I can't force them to. Highly sensitive people have a bad habit of hoping they can change toxic friends, but they just exhaust themselves in the process.

- Mixed feelings: You are going to feel guilty about abandoning the friendship. On one hand, you're unsatisfied and exhausted; on the other, you feel bad for what you're about to do. This is normal. Just don't let it sway you. It's okay to love your friend even though you know you've got to move forward.

Practice in Front of a Mirror: Don't try and end the friendship without first rehearsing what you're about to do. You won't feel confident, and you'll likely get sidetracked or derailed. Toxic people don't like admitting they're in the wrong, and they are not going to let the friendship go without a fight. Start by writing down all your thoughts. Include how the relationship makes you feel and your friend's behavior that you have previously spoken to them about. Explain why it's best to end the friendship. Once you've got everything down on paper, practice in front of a mirror until you're confident about what you want to say.

Be Direct: You can't afford to beat around the bush with toxic people—before you know it, they'll have put words in your mouth that you didn't intend to say, and you'll end up agreeing with them. Being direct will help you sever ties without any confusion.

- There is no need to be rude; just say what you've got to say in the politest way possible. Any sign of aggression can cause an unnecessary argument.

- Explain your feelings and expectations by saying something like, "I've told you before about mocking me when I say I need to leave an event early because I feel overwhelmed. But you did it again when we went out last week, and for that reason I believe it's best that I end the friendship. I feel as if you are disrespecting me as a person and refusing to accept me for who I am. I still love you, but our friendship isn't good for my mental health."

State Your Boundaries: What do you expect from your friend, moving forward? You need to make this clear so they can't say they didn't know. For example: "I will be blocking you on all social media platforms. Please don't attempt to contact me from anyone else's account. I will also erase your phone number, and I expect you to do the same. If you insist on calling, texting or sending me voice notes, I'll block you." If you have mutual friends, you may need to express these needs to them as well. For example: "I've decided I no longer want to remain friends with [state the name] any longer, for the following reasons: [state the reasons]. I would appreciate it if you don't try and contact me on their behalf, don't pass on their messages, and if there's an event or social gathering that [name of person] is going to be at, I'd rather I wasn't invited."

Fill the Void: One of the reasons toxic friends are so draining is because they take up so much of your time. Once you've ended the friendship, and you're no longer having three-hour-long conversations every night, you'll realize you've got plenty of time on your hands. You might feel confused and lonely for a while, during which time it's easy to go back to the friendship. You can prevent this by finding something else to occupy your time.

- Keep yourself distracted by finding a new hobby. You don't have to go out—teach yourself to knit, crochet, or start working on a difficult jigsaw puzzle.

- Make new friends. This might be the last thing on your mind, considering the disastrous friendship you've just come out of. But if you feel up to it, try and make some new, positive friends that will help you feel better about the friendship you've just lost. You can make new friends by volunteering, joining a club, or by going to social events.

Your Emotional Well-Being: You're not going to feel great after abandoning a toxic friendship. As a highly sensitive individual, you'll feel a lot worse than the average person. Instead of trying to suppress your feelings, deal with them as you feel them. Let your remaining friends know that you'll need them more than ever during this time. When you start feeling bad, call someone, journal, exercise, or go for a walk. However you choose to process negative feelings, take yourself through that process.

How to Set Boundaries

Setting boundaries is absolutely necessary for highly sensitive people. We attract needy people because of our natural ability to empathize. But when we allow too much access, we get overwhelmed. And while you've just read about cutting off toxic friendships, there will be some people we can't cut out of our lives, like family members and work colleagues. The only way to deal with these people is by setting boundaries.

What Are Boundaries?

Boundaries are invisible lines that the people in your life are not allowed to cross. Because they're invisible, it's up to you to let them know what they are. Think about a boundary like a front door: when it's closed, the only way for someone to get in is by knocking or ringing a bell. At that point, it's up to you to either open the door and let them in, or keep it closed. Here are some tips on how to establish boundaries with romantic partners, friends, family members and co-workers:

How to Set Boundaries With Your Partner: If you're dating someone who is not highly sensitive, they won't understand your unique needs, so you've got to explain it to them, or the relationship will fail very quickly.

- **Let Them Know You Need Alone Time:** Most people need alone time so they don't get lost in a relationship. But highly sensitive people need alone time to manage overwhelm and to recharge. Let your partner know exactly why you need to spend time alone. Explain that you do enjoy their company, but the nature of your personality means you need to isolate for a while in order to be happy. Additionally, HSPs need a strict morning routine. If you decide to move in together, or your partner stays over for the night, this needs to be explained. Let them know that the morning is your time to get your mind prepared for the day and to protect your energy; it's not something you can do together.

- **Be Direct:** Couples usually fight because of miscommunication. Let's say you've told your partner you need alone time, but you didn't explain that you need to spend time alone at least twice a week. Your boyfriend turns up on a Tuesday evening, and you tell him to leave because you need alone time. That's unfair. The reality is that the times when you will need alone time can be unpredictable, but if you know it's typically Tuesday and Thursday because those days are particularly stressful at work, you need to tell your partner this. Similarly, if you have a bad day, and you had arranged to meet your partner, call in advance and let them know you'll need to cancel because you're feeling overwhelmed and you need time to recharge.

- **Put Limits on the Relationship:** Highly sensitive people tend to attract controlling partners. This isn't always the case, but it's common. If you know your partner is slightly controlling, don't shy away from putting limits on the relationship and letting them know what you will and won't tolerate.

- **Don't Rush the Relationship:** Emotional sensitivity can make relationships difficult. You might not feel comfortable with your partner expressing their emotions too quickly, because you feel that it pressures you to do the same. It's easy for highly sensitive people to get carried away and fall in love immediately—but, as you may be aware, this generally ends in disaster. You can prevent this by telling your partner you need to take baby steps before becoming emotionally connected to someone.

- **Physical Boundaries:** Some highly sensitive people are uncomfortable with affection because it's another way they absorb energy. Too much hugging and intimacy can cause overwhelm. Let your partner know how much is too much, or if there are certain times he/she should just stay away.

- **Enforce the Consequences:** Boundaries are there for a reason. If your neighbor jumped your fence without your permission and started playing with your dog because they thought it was cute, you'd tell them to kindly not do that again—and that next time, you'll call the police! You are well within your rights to communicate the consequences for breaking the boundaries you've set. If your neighbor chose to ignore you, and you failed to enforce the consequences, you are giving them permission to continue. Similarly, if you tell your boyfriend you need alone time on Tuesdays and Thursdays but he ignores this and turns up anyway, send him home and let him know you'll be taking a one-month break from the relationship because of the violation. If he does it again, take a two-month break. During that time, you'll need to decide whether you really want to be with someone who refuses to respect your boundaries.

Creating Boundaries With Your Family: Family are the worst when it comes to setting boundaries, because they think they own you. Especially your parents! As I mentioned earlier, I've had to go no-contact with my mom and older sister. I went no-contact with my mother because she doesn't think I have the right to establish boundaries, and so she kept violating them. My sister is just toxic and refuses to change, and her continuous drama was affecting my mental health. Here are some tips on how to establish boundaries with your family:

- **Determine Your Responsibilities:** Families sometimes have unspoken rules, and everyone knows their place. The oldest sibling often takes on the responsibility of keeping things in order with the rest of the siblings. When something goes wrong, the parents will often call them and explain what's going on, which is basically their way of saying, "Sort this mess out!" As a highly sensitive person, taking on such a responsibility can be overwhelming, so it's up to you to explain this. You can say something like, "I don't mind helping out, but I would appreciate it if you didn't call me every time something goes wrong with my brothers and sisters because it's just too overwhelming for me." Or you might be the one everyone expects to hold the Thanksgiving dinner party. The next time you get the phone call informing you that you're the host, say something like, "I really appreciate the fact that everyone likes coming to mine for Thanksgiving dinner, but I find all the preparations really stressful, and I'd rather not be the host this year. If you want to have it at yours, I'm more than willing to help." In this instance, you've made your boundaries clear, but the person can't get too offended, because you've offered to help.

- **Don't Tolerate Guilt Trips:** My mother expected me to send her a monthly allowance after she retired. When I couldn't do it, she told me how all of her sisters' children were sending them money, and that she was the only one whose children were not supporting her. It worked for a while, but when the financial burden became too much for me, I put a stop to it. When a relative tries to guilt-trip you into doing something you don't want to do, say something like, "I understand how important it is that I help you out; however, it's just not in my capacity to do that right now. Furthermore, I categorically won't accept being bullied into it with your guilt trips!"

- **Explain Unacceptable Behavior:** Some parents find it difficult when their children transition into adulthood, and they'll do everything in their power to hold on to the memories that they cherish so dearly. For example, growing up, you all had dinner together every night. But now you've moved out, your parents still expect you to be at the house every evening at 7:00 p.m. for dinner!

You've been appeasing them for several months, but now it's cutting into your personal life. In this instance, try saying something like, "I really appreciate having dinner with you guys, but I can't do it every night because I've got other demands to attend to. At the moment, once a month is the best I can do." Or maybe your parents feel as if they can just stop by at your house anytime they feel like it. To establish boundaries here, you could say something like, "I'm not saying I don't want to see you guys, but could you give me at least a week's notice before making your way to my house, please?" Explain to them how intrusive it is, especially if it's your alone day. Additionally, let your parents and siblings know that you won't tolerate them judging you for the choices you make. This includes the people you date, the clothes you wear, the food you eat, etc. A parent's controlling attitude can cause major anxiety for highly sensitive people, and the only way to stop it is to tell them.

How to Establish Boundaries With Your Friends: Even if you've got a fantastic group of friends who totally understand your needs as a highly sensitive person, it's still important to set boundaries so that they are clear on acceptable behavior. Additionally, when you invite new people into your life, make sure you set boundaries from the beginning of the relationship. Here are some tips:

- **Provide Alternatives:** You will probably have a mixture of friends, some of whom are highly sensitive, and others who are not. If you're an introvert, sensitive to noise, and don't like going to bars and clubs, let your friends know that you don't mind going out, but you'd rather go to a restaurant first before the main celebration. In this way, you still get to enjoy everyone's company, and their night can still go ahead as planned, without it overwhelming you. Or if your friend has broken up with their partner and wants to come over and talk about it, agree if you know you can handle it, but be clear that they can only stay for an hour because you don't want to get overwhelmed.

- **Let Them Know You Expect Something in Return:** Life is about give and take, and as an HSP, you'll find you're always giving and not getting anything in return. Make it clear to your friends that you are not going to keep giving if it's not being returned. For example, they can't expect you to keep compromising, if they refuse to do the same. Or you might have a friend who is always hitching a free ride because they know you're going in their direction. Say something like, "I don't mind giving you a lift, but if this is going to continue, I'll need you to contribute to the gas." Maybe you have a friend who asks you to babysit every other weekend, but when you need her to return the favor, she's always conveniently busy. You can say something like, "Sorry, I can't look after your kids this week because you never look after mine. I'm going out in a couple of weeks—if you can babysit, then the next time you need me to look after your children, I'll do it."

- **Enforce Consequences:** Boundary violations are less likely to happen when you've got friends who understand your HSP needs, but every so often, you might need to put them in their place. This particularly applies to new friends. After the first violation, explain why it's unacceptable and the consequences if it happens again. For example, say you've got a friend who's always borrowing your clothes to go clubbing but returns them with cigarette burns or some other disastrous stains that you can't get rid of. But she never offers to buy the clothes back; she just returns them as if they were like that when she borrowed them. The next time she asks to borrow something, take a picture of the item and explain that there are no signs of any damage on it. If she returns it damaged, let her know you expect her to pay for it, and that she won't be borrowing any clothes from you again.

How to Set Boundaries at Work: Setting boundaries in the workplace is another difficult task. Highly sensitive people often get taken advantage of at work because we don't know how to say no. When you have unscrupulous managers or work colleagues who feel no remorse about taking your kindness for a weakness, you're going to get burned out very quickly. At my last job as an office administrator, my manager was always giving me his work to do because he knew I wouldn't say no. I always left the office an hour and a half later than everyone else, and he would saunter out of the office knowing full well that the only reason I was staying late was because I had to finish the work he'd just given me. I'd then go home crying about how my manager was taking advantage of me. My partner got sick of hearing me complain, and one day he said, "The only reason he's taking advantage of you is because you're letting him. Put your foot down. What he's asking you to do is not in your job description—he's violating the terms of your contract. You've got to say something." The next day, I did just that, and he didn't ask me to do any more extra work from then on. Here are some tips on how to set boundaries at work:

- **Be Direct:** Let me start by saying that there's absolutely no need to tell your entire office that you're highly sensitive. For one, office friends are typically never true friends—you see them Monday to Friday and that's it. Since there is no official diagnosis for high sensitivity, asking your manager to give you special treatment is unlikely to work unless you get the feeling that they're compassionate and will understand. Highly sensitive people find work environments particularly strenuous, especially when it comes to gossip. There's always that one group who sits in the break room and talks about everyone. Or the person who will get you at the water fountain and start with, "Girrrrrrl, have you heard about..." Or you can never eat your lunch in peace because Mildred has always got some complaint about the management. Unfortunately, office environments are often like high school, and the popular people are often the mean ones. The only way to deal with co-workers is to be direct. When Edna approaches you at the water fountain, say something like, "I'm sorry, Edna, but this is not my type of conversation. I'd rather not discuss other people's business." When Mildred plonks herself at your table and starts her tirade against your manager, politely state, "If you have a problem with the management, I'd rather you brought the issue to their attention. Discussing it with me is not going to resolve the matter, and it's not something I really want to hear about." For the next couple of days, you'll probably get a few dirty looks as you walk across the office, or you'll become the topic of conversation at the lunch table—but I can guarantee you, they'll stop gossiping around you for two reasons: as far as they're concerned, you're the weird one for not wanting to gossip; and they'll keep you out of their conversations because they'll be afraid you'll snitch.

- **Communicate Your Time Limits:** This is especially true when you're on a salary and don't get paid for overtime. There are some salaried employees who do so much overtime that their yearly salary amounts to as little as $15 per hour! Additionally, some managers expect to hold team meetings outside working hours via Zoom. Don't feel guilty about refusing to attend. Explain to your manager that your work starts when you get to the office, and ends when you leave. You categorically don't participate in Zoom meetings, so they'll need to brief you when you return to work. If you don't have children or you're not in a relationship, your manager might assume you've got all the time in the world to spend working, and so will expect you to take on extra shifts when no one else can. When they are short-staffed, they'll call you and ask if you can get there within the hour. It's important that you communicate your availability so you are not made to feel guilty if you can't make it. Maybe you're willing to do one extra shift per week. Let your manager know this. If he calls you outside this time, just don't answer the phone. Once you've communicated your time limits, don't budge. Clock in and clock out at the same time each day and don't make any exceptions to the rule.

- **Address Violations Immediately:** Going back to the overtime violation, say you've told your boss that you are only available for overtime on Saturday mornings, but he has taken it upon himself to call you and see if you can do the night shift because another worker didn't turn up. You understand the dilemma, but that's not your problem. First of all, you've already advised him of your availability, and nightshift wasn't on the list. Second, you specifically don't do night shifts because it messes with your sleep patterns, and you don't need that as a highly sensitive person. The next time you come into contact with your boss, ask if you can have a quiet word, and say something like, "I appreciate that you were short-staffed on Saturday night due to Daniel's unexpected absence, but I've explained that my only availability for overtime is Saturday mornings. I really felt that you overstepped the mark with this one. Can you make sure it doesn't happen again, please, or I'll stop doing overtime altogether."

- **Say "No":** Even if you want to impress your manager because you are planning on applying for a promotion or asking for a pay rise, never take on more work than you can handle. If you do so, you'll overwhelm yourself and get depressed—because, in typical HSP style, you'll have taken the world on your shoulders and will end up feeling trapped. You can avoid this by learning to say "No." Look at your workload and determine whether you can fit the extra work in or not—if you can't, say so.

- **Don't Accept an Office Cell Phone:** Some companies give their employees cell phones. It sounds like a great idea on the surface, but there are strings attached.

It basically means your manager and work colleagues can call or message you after hours, and you're obliged to respond. An office cell phone means that you never get the chance to disconnect from work. If you're offered one, decline and explain that you'd rather use your private number as a form of contact. Your manager is less likely to call you after hours on your personal line.

- **Turn Off Email Notifications:** If your work email is connected to your cell phone, turn off email notifications after hours so you're not tempted to deal with work-related issues at home.

- **Set Relationship Boundaries:** It's normal for people to date people they work with, but you've got to decide whether that's something you want to do. Having a work relationship can be especially difficult because eventually everyone will know, and they'll be all in your business. As a highly sensitive person, that's not something you need. If someone starts coming onto you in the office, let them know that you have a no-dating-at-work policy. Don't exchange numbers and take the "let's be friends" bait or you'll end up having to politely turn them down. However, if you do choose to date a colleague, establish boundaries according to what you're comfortable with. For example, you might be okay with dating someone if they're prepared to keep your relationship a secret, or maybe you don't mind people knowing, but you're not into public displays of affection.

- **Be Careful When Sharing Your Beliefs/Affiliations:** Religion and politics are two subjects that can cause major conflicts amongst people who are passionate about their beliefs. Instead of getting into heated debates, explain that you're not interested in discussing such topics. You'll find that tensions rise during election time, and everyone wants to know whose side you're on. That's none of anyone's concern, and you are well within your rights to withhold such information.

- **Know Your Emotional Boundaries:** Get to know your colleagues in a professional and open manner, but it's important to find the right balance so that you're not too professional, and you're not too open. Once you've found that balance, make sure it's maintained. If you feel that a colleague is asking you too many personal questions or being overbearing and invading your space, tell them. Some people are naturally very open, and they assume everyone else is too. The only way to make someone aware they're violating your boundaries is to tell them. Ask the person to have a quiet chat and say something like, "I'm really glad you feel comfortable being so open with me; however, I'm more of a private person and I'd rather not share that kind of information with the people I work with. I would appreciate it if you didn't ask me questions of that nature again."

Just Say No: Today, "No" is the most important word in my vocabulary. I used to hate it, and said "Yes" to everything but couldn't understand why I was so overwhelmed all the time. When wielded in the right way, "No" is a shield against exploitation and an instrument of integrity. It's a word that's difficult to receive, and takes courage to say, but it sets us free from the demands of others.

We love the word "Yes"—it supports boldness, risk-taking, and to those who love to use it, displays their open-hearted approach to life. I am in no way attempting to minimize the grace that is found in "Yes," but "No" is the protective force that creates a barrier between the influence of others and self. We don't like celebrating the word "No," but it's a hidden power that's completely misunderstood. Most people are unaware of the strength we draw from "No" because society has labelled it as something negative. But we've got it all wrong. Negativity is shrouded in naysaying and energy draining. Negative people don't inspire others to take action; instead they strangle their enthusiasm. There is nothing powerful about negativity—when you are around it, you feel miserable. Negativity is a persistent attitude, but "No" is a choice you make based on the options you've been given. It announces to your audience that you are not co-signing because it's not your truth. "I will not read over your essay, look after your children, or join your association, because I am committed to my own goals. You can strike me off that list because I don't want to jump on that bandwagon; I do not agree, and I'm not comfortable with it. I'm grateful for the invite, and I'm sorry if you feel hurt, but my needs are more important."

The word "No" is a badge of personal responsibility. It says that, although we have friends and loved ones, and we value and respect those relationships, we can't allow them to control and influence us. "No" is both the barrier and the tool we use to draw and maintain a perimeter around ourselves. "No" says that you can only come so far because I have chosen to maintain a distance between you and my needs. "No" sets us apart from friends and family; it lets them know that, although I support you, this is the space I've carved out for myself, and it's going to stay this way until I decide otherwise.

To make this easier, think about the word "No" from a child's perspective. If you've ever tried to tell a two-year-old what to eat, what to wear, or when to stop playing with their toys, you'll know that if they don't want to do it, they are going to scream and holler "No!" Why? Because they feel as if their boundaries are being violated, and they are being forced to do something they don't want to do. Despite the fact that the child is under the guardianship of his parents, they are already trying to establish their independence and break away from the constraints of their mom and dad. When it comes to saying "No," we need to take a leaf out of the two-year-old's book. If it doesn't feel right, if it's a violation of your boundaries, if you've got more important things to do—say "No."

Limit Your Communication: I will start with the phone. Smartphones were once a dreaded curse for me. I had a love-hate relationship with my cell phone. Love because it alleviated my boredom, but hate because social media became addictive, and it gave people too much access to me. However, things changed once I learned how to set boundaries. Let me start by explaining how social media can affect highly sensitive people:

- **It Provides Too Much Stimulation:** Highly sensitive people notice everything and then spend time in deep thought about the information. This means it's easy to get overstimulated, and this manifests in difficulty concentrating, irritability, anxiety, stomachache, or some other uncomfortable feeling. Social media provides even more information for our brains to process, which adds to our stimulation.

- **It Triggers Empathy:** There were times when I'd see things on social media that made me so sad. One of the worst was a video about a little girl dying from an incurable disease. It was so heartbreaking that I spent the entire weekend depressed because of it. I was constantly having an emotional response to the things I saw on social media, and it had a terrible effect on my mental health. A casual scroll through Facebook would often turn into a crying fest. Most of the time, if I was feeling stressed and started scrolling to get some relief, I would end up worse than when I started.

- **It Leads to the Fear of Missing Out:** Despite the fact that highly sensitive people don't like being around people who gossip and have insincere conversations, we still experience the fear of missing out when we go through other people's social media pages. Online, it looks like everyone is having so much fun. As an HSP, you are more likely to spend the weekend in front of the TV than going to the work leaving do. Or reading a book under the duvet instead of going to lunch with friends. When you check your social media and everyone's posting pictures of the blast they've just had, it can make you feel like your life isn't enough, and that since your life isn't enough, you're not enough. Hands up anyone who can resonate with this feeling.

- **It Leads to Unnecessary Arguments:** We live in a black or white world—you are either on one side or the other. If you don't say anything, you're guilty of not being a part of the solution. As a result, it can be very easy to get into unnecessary arguments on social media. If people don't agree with your opinion, instead of having an intelligent discussion about the topic, they'll often insult you. Many people take things the wrong way and get offended over something that wasn't intended to cause offense. Sometimes, you just can't win on social media. Someone will say something rude, you respond—and the next thing you know, you've got World War III on your hands.

How to Deal With Social Media: Put limits on how much you use it—or don't use it at all. Here are a few tips:

- Delete your social media profiles.
- Remove temptation by using an app blocker.
- Don't follow accounts that don't express your values or that trigger you.
- Be strategic about your social media use—only log on when you are looking for something in particular.
- Set limits on how long you spend on social media and who you interact with.
- Replace your social media apps with mindfulness tools to use during your downtime.

Do Not Disturb: Every day we are bombarded with information from different sources—social media, WhatsApp, email, Snapchat, and random apps that we've downloaded. So much of our time is either spent trying to shut out the noise or keep up with the endless conversations we are forced to have. Studies have found that notification-based anxiety has become an epidemic in America. One teacher reported that one of her students received more than 150 Snapchat notifications in an hour! A study conducted by Harvard University on the relationship between smartphone use and the feel-good hormone dopamine found that smartphones have given us access to an endless supply of positive and negative social stimuli. No matter what type of notification you get, whether it's an Instagram like or a text message from the guy you have a crush on, the positive social stimuli triggers a dopamine release. Experts state that the frequent vibrations and pings from our phones interfere with our ability to focus and get stuff done. As mentioned, dopamine is a feel-good hormone; when the brain experiences it, it wants to stay there. That's why you can spend hours scrolling on social media—you're looking for something to stimulate your mind so you can get the next dopamine hit. It's the reason why comedy, gossip pages and accounts that are visually appealing do so well on social media. People need a constant stream of entertainment to feed their dopamine habit.

For the average person, notification overload can become overwhelming and can cause anxiety. But it is particularly detrimental for highly sensitive people and can cause an endless cycle of depression. The good news is that you can free yourself from notification syndrome by putting your phone on DO NOT DISTURB (DND)—that's if you've got an iPhone! Apple introduced this feature in 2012. It was originally designed for users to silence their phones during the night. But a lot of people, myself included, have their phones on DND at all times. You will find it in your settings, and you can set it to keep your phone on silent during certain times, or all the time. If there are people you want to be able to reach you when they need to, you can add them to your favorites, and they can get through at any time.

I keep my phone on DND at all times, and it's amazing. It means I can screen my calls and messages and reply if and when I want to. It literally feels as if I don't have a phone—I'm in full control of who I respond to, and I'll call people back in my own time. Let me warn you, a lot of your friends and family members are going to get offended when you put your phone on DND because they are used to having access to you whenever they want. Now, they'll feel like they literally have to book an appointment if they want to speak to you. Some of your friends will fall off because of it—mine did. But I wasn't concerned because they were the ones who had narcissistic traits. They abandoned the friendship because I had cut off their supply. Your true friends will stick around because they'll understand why you're doing it. It's not because you're being rude and disrespectful; you are highly sensitive and you don't need the overstimulation. It's as simple as that. Anyone who doesn't understand, you don't need in your life!

How to Make Deeper Connections With People

Unfortunately, we live in a very superficial world where surface-level conversations are the norm. Try and go any deeper, and people think you're weird! But for me, deep conversations are food for my soul. Even though I'm an introvert who rejuvenates best alone, I've met some rare people who give me energy. I'm refreshed by people who can talk to me about passions, dreams, intentions or feelings. When I'm engaged with a person like this, you would assume I'm a very talkative person. On the other hand, I can't stand small talk. Where I got my shoes, the latest reality show, the weather, my weekend… These skimming-the-water conversations make me very uncomfortable, and I can come across as very unsociable when I'm forced to converse with people about such things. This type of conversation lets me know that the person I'm speaking to is trapped in the cycle of politeness and niceties. It gives me the same feeling

I get when I go to Starbucks: they're only making small talk because that's what they've been trained to do.

Why HSPs Crave Deeper Connections

I went through a phase in my life where I could only socialize when I was well and truly drunk. I just couldn't do it sober, and for many years believed I suffered from antisocial personality disorder. I hated going to work functions, networking events or any other type of social gathering because I'd spend the whole night repeating the same introduction I'd rehearsed on my way there and having similar conversations with different people. It was like they were robots. If dinner was involved, I got really tense at the table, and found myself trying to tune into one of the many conversations that were taking place around me. I felt overstimulated because too much was going on at once, and the small talk didn't make things any better.

Because highly sensitive people feel emotions on a deeper level, the connections we make either drain us or feed us. When we have shallow connections, we end up exhausted. Even if you've got 5000 friends on Facebook and people blowing up your phone all the time, you will still feel lonely because you're not craving a lot of friends—you're craving *connection*. If this is resonating with you, it might be time to start thinking about the friendships you've made. Which ones drain you, and which ones feed you? In general, if you want deeper connections, you'll need to go out and make them. You'll find that some people are superficial because they're just trying to fit in with everyone else. But deep down, they're desperate to find someone they can express their true feelings with. Here are some tips on how you can make deeper connections with your friends, family members, co-workers, neighbors, and the people you meet on a day-to-day basis:

Ask More Intense Questions: We've been conditioned to believe that small talk is polite, but who says you've got to follow the rules?

- Instead of asking, "How are you?" ask, "How are you feeling?"

- Ask about the struggles they've had to deal with recently.

- Find out a person's true intentions by asking, "Why?"

- If you feel uncomfortable that the conversation isn't moving forwards, encourage the person to speak by asking, "What are your thoughts on this?"

I never used to feel confident enough to take the lead and deepen the conversation. My anxiety always got the better of me, and I listened to the voice in my head telling me I would sound like an idiot so it was best that I kept my mouth shut. Once I got over that, I realized that highly sensitive people also have the power to take a conversation to the next level. There is no point in complaining that people are too superficial if we don't take the initiative to find out if there is more to someone's character than they are revealing. What I found was that there are a lot of people waiting to be asked them the right questions so they know it's safe enough to reveal how they really feel. To my surprise, some of the people I assumed were extremely superficial had a lot more depth to them than I thought.

Tune Into What Others Are Feeling: Sometimes, it can feel like a person has lost interest in the conversation. We automatically jump to the conclusion that we were the offending party, which makes us feel awful. But it might be that they're just having a bad day. In situations like this, use your HSP superpowers to discern what's really going on. Remember, we have the ability to absorb emotions. You might sense worry, or fear. Use how you're feeling as a marker and ask how they are feeling. If they are going through an emotionally challenging situation, you can be that listening ear. I often find that when I ask someone how they're feeling, they tell me—because most people are not comfortable with lying. Additionally, the fact that you've asked how they are feeling is an indication that you can tell something is not quite right.

Use Small Talk as a Stepping Stone: Some people will want to find out more about you, but they won't want to cross boundaries. You can use small talk to reveal more about yourself; for example, when someone asks, "How was your weekend?" you can say something like, "It was great. I'm writing a book about how to regulate your emotions, and I got a lot done over the weekend. I learned a lot of really interesting stuff while I was researching the topic." At this point, they will either ask you to elaborate, or they'll give you more information about what *they* got up to over the weekend. In this way, you are letting the person know what you value and who you are, which will lead to a deeper conversation.

Practice Being Honest: In his book *Radical Honesty*, author Brad Blanton writes about a concept called "radical honesty." We live in a world where we've been told that it's not safe to talk about your feelings unless you can trust the person you're communicating with. But Blanton believes this is the wrong way to go about connecting with people. Radical honesty involves speaking the truth at all times and avoiding the white lies we typically tell. When we avoid the truth, we get entangled in a web of deceit, but when we are honest, we reveal our authentic selves and give other people the opportunity to understand us better. Here is what radical honesty might look like:

- "I'm not ready to go to an event like that, especially when I don't know anyone."
- "I find this difficult to admit, but..."
- "I'm finding it hard to concentrate on what's being said right now."
- "I need XYZ to be comfortable in certain situations."

Highly sensitive people have a habit of carrying the weight of the world on their shoulders because we don't want to offend anyone. But you will find that life becomes a lot simpler when you start unapologetically speaking the truth.

I have suffered from depression my entire life; I didn't understand why until I found out that I was highly sensitive. However, now I know how to manage it because I have been given the right tools, and in Chapter 7, I'll be giving those same tools to you.

CHAPTER 7:

DEALING WITH DEPRESSION AS A HIGHLY SENSITIVE PERSON

I met depression for the first time when I was 13 years old. My parents took me to a therapist because I was always crying and spent most of my time alone. I was diagnosed with clinical depression and put on antidepressants. The medication just numbed my feelings and helped me bury my emotions further. I stopped taking them when I was 18 and got acquainted with destructive coping mechanisms such as smoking marijuana and drinking alcohol. It wasn't until years later that I found out why I was so prone to depression. Highly sensitive people are vulnerable to depression because when our nervous systems get overstimulated, it is exhausting and stressful. When we don't know how to manage our high sensitivity, we remain in a state of overstimulation, which can cause depression. We are also adversely affected by other people's moods, environmental stressors, diet, hormonal shifts, and medication. All of these things can have a profound effect on us and make us more vulnerable to depression. Additionally, highly sensitive people have stronger emotional reactions than the average person. When we feel bad, we feel terrible, and will often spiral into depression as a result.

Pay Attention to Symptoms of Depression

I used to go through intense depressive episodes because I just allowed myself to get lost in my feelings. But now I know how to monitor my symptoms and control them so I don't end up unable to get out of bed for two weeks. Here are some typical symptoms that will let you know you are about to experience a depressive episode:

- Fatigue or loss of energy
- Feelings of excessive guilt or worthlessness
- Indecisiveness or difficulty concentrating
- Decreased movement
- Increased agitation
- Disrupted sleep
- A loss of appetite causing weight loss

Refrain From Isolation: Although highly sensitive people need to recharge in isolation, isolating during a depressive episode is not a good idea. Research suggests that loneliness and isolation is linked to mental and physical health conditions such as cardiovascular disease and an increased risk of early death. A study conducted in 2018 discovered that social isolation and loneliness affects sleep quality. Other studies have found links between anxiety, depression, and social disconnectedness. In other words, the more you isolate yourself when you're depressed, the more depressed you'll feel.

Stick to Your Daily Routine: In earlier chapters, you read about the importance of having a strict daily routine. It's particularly important to stick to this when you start feeling depressed. If you don't, you'll find that days turn into weeks, and weeks turn into months; you'll lose track of time and forget to prioritize self-care. Sticking to your routine will:

- Remind you that every morning is the beginning of a new day
- Keep you focused on healthy habits like exercising and getting a full night's sleep
- Give you something to look forward to like listening to inspirational music while you're having breakfast.

Start a Project That Makes You Happy: Turn your depression into something positive by diving into a home project or a hobby that you haven't engaged with in a while. Studies suggest that crafting, gardening, and creating art can all help to soothe stress.

Reverse Dysfunctional Thinking

Dysfunctional thinking involves framing the world through a lens that makes it appear as if you're fighting a never-ending battle that you can't win. Here are a few examples:

- **Labeling:** Defining yourself by your mistakes. If you've been divorced, you'll think things like, "No one will ever want me because I've been divorced." Or, "I'm such a failure; I'm so unworthy that my husband divorced me."
- **Minimization and Magnification:** Brushing important issues under the carpet and refusing to acknowledge them. Or making minor problems appear larger than they are.
- **"Should" Statements:** Using words such as "should," "ought," and "must" is a form of negative self-judgment.

- **Emotional Reasoning:** Thinking with your emotions or allowing your emotions to affect how you see things.

- **Blaming:** Blaming yourself when you are not responsible.

- **Overgeneralization:** Thinking that all your experiences are going to be bad because you had one negative experience.

- **Mind-Reading:** Thinking that you know what's going through a person's mind, or that you are responsible for someone's negative emotions.

- **Fortune-Telling:** Assuming you can foretell the future based on random events.

- **Discounting or Filtering the Positives:** Refusing to acknowledge the positive aspects of the situation and only focusing on the negatives.

- **Polarized Thinking:** This is also known as "black-and-white" thinking, and it involves refusing to acknowledge the gray areas of a situation.

Write Out Your Automatic Thoughts: Automatic thoughts are the ideas that randomly pop into your head. They tend to focus on three areas: thoughts about yourself; thoughts about the future; and thoughts about the world. Once you've identified why your mood changed, you can look at how your automatic thoughts relate to the event. You can then determine if the thoughts are dysfunctional, and if so, challenge them, looking for evidence that either confirms or disagrees with the thought. Take the following steps to evaluate your automatic thoughts:

- Get a journal, divide one page into four sections, and write one word in each section: event; feelings; automatic thought; dysfunctional thought. Here's an example: *Event:* I was stuttering during my presentation. *Feelings:* I was embarrassed. *Automatic thought:* Everyone thinks you're stupid. *Dysfunctional thought:* Labeling yourself. Here's another example: *Event:* The conversation fizzled out at Sophie's party. *Feeling:* I felt as if everyone was trying to avoid me. *Automatic thoughts:* They think I'm an idiot—that's why no one wants to speak to me. *Dysfunctional thought:* Mind-reading.

- Now replace your automatic thoughts with thoughts that are more rational and reasonable. Here is an example: *Event:* I was stuttering during my presentation. *Feelings:* I was embarrassed. *Automatic thought:* Everyone thinks you're stupid. *Dysfunctional thought:* Labeling yourself. *Rational Thought:* This label doesn't define me; nobody thinks I'm stupid; I'll make improvements for my next presentation.

Structure Your Day: Feeling as if you've got no control over your life intensifies feelings of depression. You can overcome this by knowing exactly what you're going to be doing throughout the day. When you know you've got things to do, your brain goes into action mode to get them done. When you're lulling about not sure of your next move, you spend your time in rumination. Rumination is where you replay a problem or a scenario over and over in your head without coming to a viable solution or conclusion. Continuously thinking about your situation just adds to the depression. You can either use a productivity app or write it down, but plan out every hour of your day so you know exactly what you're doing from one moment to the next.

Identify Your Feelings During an Activity: Write about how you felt as you performed each activity during your day. Did you experience any pleasure? Did you feel sad? What emotions if any did you feel? Try not to evaluate your activities on an "all or nothing" scale; instead, use a scale of 1-10, with ten being the maximum, and one being the minimum.

Find Distractions For Overwhelm: When you are experiencing intense emotions or rumination, a distraction causes you to focus your attention on something else so you snap out of it. Here are some examples:

- Meditation
- Prayer
- Reading a book
- Dancing
- Playing with a pet

It is important to mention that depression is a serious condition. While the above tips have been extremely helpful for me, if you find that your depression has become so overwhelming that you can't manage it, it's essential that you get professional help.

Anxiety is another mental health issue that highly sensitive people are prone to. The good news is that there are a wide range of strategies you can implement in your life to overcome it. I will discuss them further in Chapter 8.

CHAPTER 8:

DEALING WITH ANXIETY AS A HIGHLY SENSITIVE PERSON

Anxiety is how the body responds to stress. It's a natural emotion that's characterized by a fear of the future. It's normal for people to feel anxious during major life-changing events such as getting married, having children, changing jobs, or moving to another country. Anxious feelings make us aware of the risks we are facing and alert us if we are in a dangerous or a difficult situation. This is referred to as the fight-or-flight response. The brain responds to danger or threat by releasing stress hormones such as cortisol and adrenaline. But once the situation has been resolved, the body returns to its natural state. Even if there is no real threat, these hormones still cause the body to experience anxiety-related symptoms.

However, anxiety becomes a problem when the symptoms are extreme and they last for extended periods of time. In this case, you may have an anxiety disorder. According to the American Psychiatric Association, approximately 40 million adults living in the United States suffer from an anxiety disorder, and more women are diagnosed with the condition than men. Here are some of the symptoms you may experience if you're feeling anxious:

- Dissociation
- A desire to escape the situation
- A change in appetite
- Sleep problems
- Heightened alertness
- Irritability
- Feelings of panic, dread, or impending doom
- Difficulty concentrating
- Uncontrollable overthinking
- Racing thoughts
- Stomachache and nausea
- Dizziness and fainting
- A lack of energy and extreme tiredness
- Increased heartbeat
- Hair loss
- Shaking
- Dry mouth
- Blushing or hot flushes
- Fast and heavy breathing
- Sweating

Life moves at lightning speed. Some people enjoy this way of living—fast-paced, busy ,and flying from one activity to the next. But this is not the case for highly sensitive people. We find it stressful and challenging for our mental health. Emotions such as anxiety, loneliness, and fear can quickly invade our lives. Because we feel things so intensely, these emotions can completely overwhelm us and can become very distressing. Once anxiety takes over, it can feel as if there's no turning back and that the black hole that's swallowing you will totally consume you. Unfortunately, there is no permanent cure for anxiety; you will always find yourself in situations that are going to make you feel anxious. The good news is that there are strategies you can implement to eliminate feelings of anxiety when they show up. Here is what works best for me:

BREATHING EXERCISES

Breathing is one of the body's many automatic functions, and because it's automatic, we often pay no attention to it, but the reality is that the majority of us don't breathe properly. Most of us have developed poor breathing habits, and two of the main reasons for this are bad posture and fast-paced living. As a result, shallow breathing has become the norm. If you have a baby, pay attention to the way they breathe—it's slow and deep. If you don't have children, observe the way *you* breathe when you feel relaxed. You will notice that your breathing is calm and slow. The best time to monitor this is first thing in the morning and before you go to bed at night.

The problem with shallow breathing is that you're only filling a small portion of your lungs, and this has a negative effect on your cell metabolism, focus, and other bodily functions. Let's take a look at some of the negative effects of shallow breathing:

THE NEGATIVE EFFECTS OF SHALLOW BREATHING

- **Impairs Cognitive Function:** A study conducted by researchers at Northwestern University discovered a link between cognitive function and breathing. This link becomes stronger during inhalation because shallow breathing disrupts the balance of carbon dioxide and oxygen. It prevents the right amount of oxygen entering the body, and the right amount of carbon dioxide from leaving the body. When the body is not getting enough oxygen, it affects your ability to think.

- **Increases Blood Pressure:** Shallow breathing increases the heart rate and therefore increases blood pressure. Longer, deeper breaths decrease blood pressure by slowing the heart rate.

- **Impairs Physical Ability:** Shallow breathing prevents the body from fully using its respiratory muscles. Deep breathing is a form of exercise for the abdominal and diaphragm muscles. Weak respiratory muscles result in impaired physical ability and endurance.

The Benefits of Deep Breathing

Not only does proper breathing relieve anxiety, it also has several other health benefits. Here are some of them:

- **Relieves Anxiety:** Anxiety causes shallow breathing, which raises blood pressure and causes rapid breathing. But deep breathing sends a message to the brain to calm down, and the brain then sends a message to the body to relax. As a result, the heart rate slows and blood pressure decreases.

- **Strengthens the Lungs:** Breathing exercises increase the lungs' elasticity, which creates more space to hold more air. As a result, the lungs become stronger.

- **Strengthens the Body:** When there is more oxygen in the cells, muscles and joints become stronger. The body is protected against the physical strain of exercise, and this prevents wear and tear of the muscles.

- **Reduces Inflammation:** Proper breathing cools the body down, which reduces inflammation in the digestive system.

- **Glowing, Healthy Skin:** When the oxygen concentration in the cells increases, it improves the texture of the skin. Breathing the right way also helps regulate hormones, which reduces stress, leading to clearer skin.

- **Improves Cognitive Function:** As mentioned, when the brain lacks oxygen, our thinking capabilities are impaired. However, proper breathing provides the brain with the oxygen it needs for optimal memory, concentration, and focus.

- **Cardiovascular Health:** Breathing exercises improve blood pressure and strengthen cardiovascular muscles. Proper breathing stimulates the vagus nerve, which deactivates the fight-or-flight response. All these reduce your chances of having a stroke.

- **Improves Digestive System:** The digestive system needs oxygen to function at its best. Proper breathing helps resolve gastrointestinal problems such as indigestion and constipation.

- **Eliminates Toxins:** Shallow breathing keeps the body in an acidic state, but deep breathing helps to expel toxins from the body, which in turn keeps the body in a healthier alkaline state.

- **Improves Sleep Quality:** Deep breathing relaxes the body, which helps you to sleep better.

- You can practice breathing exercises at any time, and you don't need any special equipment or tools to do so. There are several breathing exercises you can do to relax when you are feeling anxious. However, the aim is to get into the habit of breathing properly all the time; you can achieve this by practicing breathing exercises twice a day. I do them first thing in the morning, and just before I go to sleep, and I find that deep breathing helps me fall asleep faster.

BELLY BREATHING

- Lie flat on your back or sit in a comfortable position.

- Place your left hand on your stomach just underneath your rib cage, and your right hand on your chest.

- Take a deep breath in through your nose, and allow your stomach to expand outwards. Your chest should remain still.

- Purse your lips and breathe out in a whistling motion. Your stomach will sink inwards. Use your hand to push all the air out.

- Repeat the exercise 10 times.

- Pay attention to the way you feel at the end of the exercise.

4-7-8 Breathing

Stick with belly breathing until you've mastered it before moving on to 4-7-8 breathing because it's slightly more advanced.

- Sit or lie in a comfortable position, place your left hand on your belly under your rib cage, and your right hand on your chest.
- Breathe in deeply from your stomach. As you breathe in, count to 4.
- Once you get to 4, hold your breath and count to 7.
- Exhale fully while counting to 8, making sure that all the air has left your lungs.
- Repeat the exercise 7 times, or as many times as you need to feel calm.
- Pay attention to the way you feel at the end of the exercise.

Roll Breathing

Again, this is a more advanced breathing exercise, and it helps you use the full capacity of your lungs and focus on your breathing rhythm. While you are practicing, you should perform roll breathing lying on your back with your knees bent. But once you are used to it, you can do the exercise in any position.

- Put your right hand on your chest, and your left hand on your stomach. As you breathe in and out, pay attention to the way your hands move.
- Fill your lower lungs with air by taking a slow, deep breath. Always inhale through your nose, and exhale through your mouth. Do this 10 times.

- Take a deep breath into your lower lungs and breathe in further into your upper chest. Breathe regularly and slowly.

- Breathe out through your mouth and make a quiet whooshing sound. Feel the tension leaving your body as you start to relax.

- Practice breathing like this for 5 minutes.

- Pay attention to the way you feel after the exercise.

How to Mindfully Control Anxiety

In a mindful state, you create space to reflect, step back, and respond thoughtfully instead of reacting spontaneously to the things that trigger anxiety in you. I found that mindfulness came easily to me, and many other HSPs I know have said the same thing. The main reason for this is that mindfulness involves reflection, and highly sensitive people are naturally reflective. Nevertheless, the challenge is remembering to step into it when you need to. Combining the magic of spirituality and the science of psychology, here are some tips on how to banish your anxiety with mindfulness:

Embrace Your Emotions: Highly sensitive people are often made to feel ashamed of their emotions because they feel them more deeply than others do. We are often told that we're exaggerating or too sensitive. Well, they have one thing right—we *are* too sensitive, just not in the way they think. As a result of these comments, many highly sensitive people have learned to bury their emotions out of fear of being judged. I learned to do this as a child because my parents and siblings couldn't understand why I reacted so strongly to things, and I was often punished for showing emotions such as fear, anger, or sadness. But emotions are designed to be felt, and ignoring them only causes an explosion later, or, even worse, an emotional meltdown. Treat yourself with the same kindness you would an overwhelmed friend. Would you tell them to "Shut up and stop being silly?" Or would you sit with them and help them talk through their emotions? Here are some tips on how you can embrace your emotions:

- Highly sensitive people generally feel emotions as physical sensations. Gain full awareness of the emotion you're feeling by locating it in your body. You might feel it as muscle tension in your back or shoulders, shortness of breath, or a stomachache.

- Don't ignore the emotion—sit with it. Experts suggest that emotions such as anger pass within 90 seconds. Depending on what you're feeling, it might take longer for highly sensitive people. But that's okay. Take as long as you need.

- Remember that difficult emotions act as messengers; they are alerting you to what's going on inside or around you so you can address it before something bad happens.

Label Your Emotions: When I got married, I felt terrible anxiety and anger that I now had to share my life with someone else. I was used to being independent, traveling when I wanted to, cooking and cleaning for myself, and making important decisions alone. Now I had to consult another person about every aspect of my life. What made matters worse was that he didn't understand my high sensitivity. He does now, but back then, I was thinking about divorce every other day. Through therapy, I learned to acknowledge and label my emotions to prevent them from taking over my life. I had to cultivate the habit of asking myself how I felt: "Am I feeling resentful, angry, ashamed, or sad?" It's also important to mention that even though you're highlighting the emotion, you are not the emotion, and it doesn't define you. "I am depressed" and "I am feeling depressed" are two different states of being. "I am depressed" is connected to your identity; "I am feeling depressed" is a feeling that will eventually pass.

I would listen to how I was feeling, label the emotion, and then say, "I am feeling tense and frustrated right now, and it's okay to feel this way. I am just going to sit with the feeling until it passes." Don't get me wrong—sometimes my bad feelings took a while to go away, and sometimes it would take days or weeks before my anxiety subsided. But labeling my feelings allowed me to stop being *afraid* of what I was feeling.

Feelings Don't Last Forever: When you are in a state of anxiety, it's easy to believe that the feeling will last forever. But emotions are not permanent; you can experience a range of emotions in 24 hours. I started seeing my emotions as clouds that float through the sky—you can watch them pass by, change shape, and disappear into obscurity. When it comes to your emotions, act like an observer at all times and process them with love and kindness. Ask yourself:

- "What do I need to feel better right now?"
- "What can I do to nurture myself?"
- "What is the nicest thing I can do for myself right now?"

What is the Root Cause? Evaluating where the negative emotion originated from will enable you to evaluate it from a critical standpoint and get a better understanding of what you're experiencing. Take some time out to explore and reflect on the situation that caused the negative emotion in the first place. Maybe you are feeling disconnected, unappreciated, or angry with a romantic partner, friend, or co-worker. Ask yourself:

- "Why am I feeling this way? Is it because of what somebody said? Or because of what someone did or didn't do?"

Don't just walk through the emotion—explore it, and make space to get some authentic answers.

Don't Try and Control How You Feel: Let go of the need to fix or control how you feel. I used to tell myself how much better I'd feel if the negative emotions just disappeared because I hated the way they made me feel. But you don't need to hurry through negative emotions; they're not going to kill you. As I'm sure you're aware, you'll be okay once you get to the other side. Anxiety is definitely uncomfortable, and it's one emotion I wish I didn't have to feel, but as author and therapist Katherine Woodward Thomas says, "You won't find the answers to the difficult questions in life running from your problems. Sometimes you've got to sit in the mess of humanity powerless to tidy it all up to find wisdom." Trying to micromanage our souls disrupts the order of life. Nature has an inborn intelligence, so let the wisdom of the universe play her role. Leave your messy emotions alone, be patient with them, and trust that every life force on the planet is supporting your evolution. As I have experienced, embracing your pain will guide you in the direction of deeper insight and true joy.

Mantra Meditations: Saying a mantra while you meditate is a great way to control anxiety, relieve stress, and release pressure. Additionally, research has found that it improves your health, productivity and happiness. Just meditating for five minutes per day will provide you with a deeper level of inner peace, and improve your creativity and relationships. This guided meditation really helps with my anxiety. It gave me an immediate feeling of calm, harmony, satisfaction, and centeredness. I hope it helps relieve your anxiety too. Here are the steps:

- Set an alarm on your phone for 5 minutes.

- Sit in a comfortable position with your back straight and your legs crossed.

- Make an "O" shape by placing the tip of your index finger and your thumb together while leaving your other three fingers straight. Rest your hands on top of your knees.

- Take slow, deep breaths. On the inhale, say in your mind, "Breathe in forgiveness, love, peace." On the exhale, say, "Breathe out everything that doesn't serve me."

- Continue taking deep breaths and stretch your arms upwards while you breathe in. Lengthen your spine while you breathe out.

Anxiety Triggers For Highly Sensitive People

As mentioned, we will never fully escape anxiety because we are always going to encounter stressful events in life. However, highly sensitive people are more prone to anxiety than others, and it's important to know what triggers it so you can do your best to avoid those things. Everyone is different, but in general, I have found that there are some common denominators that trigger anxiety in HSPs:

- **Overscheduling:** When I can plan ahead, and I more or less know the outcome of a situation, I can handle having several items on my to-do list. But when I'm all over the place, and I don't really understand what's going on because I've taken on too much, I get really anxious. Learning how to say "No" was one of my biggest blessings in life.

- **A Harsh Environment:** I was once forced to sit in the audience of *American Idol* to support a friend of a friend. It was terrible, especially when the audience started booing, or the judges were overly critical. Everyone else thought it was funny, but it made me feel awful.

- **Other People's Anger:** When people get angry, it makes me anxious, even if it has nothing to do with me. The emotion is a very strong one, and when I'm around it, I get anxious.

- **Violence and Horror in Movies:** I don't bother going to the movies anymore, not even to watch cartoons, because I never leave feeling good. There's always something that startles me.

- **Strong Smells:** Some essential oils are good for anxiety, but if you're sensitive to smells, it's not a good idea to use them. The same applies to perfume.

- **Being the Host:** I hate hosting social events; I get terribly overwhelmed and anxious. It starts with paranoia that no one's going to turn up, then when they do, I get anxious that people aren't enjoying themselves. I just don't host events anymore.

- **Artificial Lights:** We can't really get away from artificial lights; they're all over the place. I spend a lot of time in hats and sunglasses to protect me from them.

- **Loud TV or Music:** In general, I can't handle loud noise, whether it's from a TV, radio, or any other device. I do most of my shopping online to avoid going to malls and grocery stores where it can get pretty loud.

- **Disorder and Chaos:** Clutter and disorder is disastrous for me. I work from home, and when things are out of order, I can't focus. I've tried working from co-working spaces and libraries, and even though they are relatively quiet environments, all the walking around, tapping on keyboards and whispering was too much for me.

- **Trivial Conversations:** I get anxious during small talk because I'm afraid the person I'm speaking to can see that I'm not interested in the conversation. I also get anxious because I find it so difficult to engage in small talk and don't really know what to say.

- **Negative People:** You can choose your friends, but you can't choose your friends' friends. I get anxious when I know I'm going to meet new people just in case they're a negative Nancy or a negative Nigel.

- **Confrontation:** There are some people who are just confrontational; they have a problem for every solution and want to argue about everything. Confrontation makes me uncomfortable, so when I notice this character trait in a person, I quickly distance myself from them.

- **Having Guests in Your Home:** As mentioned, my mother once spent an entire year at my house, and it was hands down the worst year of my life! I can deal with having people in my space for a day or two, but anything longer than that triggers severe anxiety in me.

- **Too Many People:** One of the main reasons I don't go to parties, concerts, and other events where there are crowds is because I get overwhelmed by all the energy and noise.

- **Bright Lights:** Bright lights make me very uncomfortable; they give me an immediate headache, and I lose focus.

There is more to living a fulfilled life as a highly sensitive person than overcoming the negative effects of this trait. It's time to take things to the next level. In Chapter 9, you will find out how.

CHAPTER 9:

IN THE PURSUIT OF WHOLENESS

Take a moment and think about what wholeness looks like to you... It's important that you define wholeness for yourself, or you'll end up chasing what doesn't truly fulfil you. It's easy to get caught up in society's definition of wholeness. We are constantly bombarded with messages telling us what we need in order to be fulfilled. A great career, a nice house, a nice car, an attractive partner, money in the bank and a vacation home. If we don't have these things, we are indirectly told we're defective in some way. But it's clear that living just to gain material wealth doesn't satisfy—the rich and famous tell us this all the time. The very people we are trying to emulate are telling us that real happiness comes from within. And your "within" is very personal to you. However, in order to reach that state of complete wholeness, there is a foundation you need so you can build on it. Here my three foundations of happiness:

A Clear Sense of Purpose: The combination of a loving family, a successful career, and meaningful relationships might sound like the recipe for the ideal life. But I've often found that people who can check all these boxes still feel a void in their lives, and that void is purpose. There is more to purpose than a cliché or a distant dream that you'll never attain, and it is not merely the reserve of a few special people in the world. We all have a purpose. Everyone was put on the earth to make an impact. Research has found that purpose is a tool for a healthier and happier life that very few people attempt to use. According to a study reported in *The New York Times*, approximately 25% of American adults state that they have a clear sense of purpose, and this is what makes their lives meaningful—while 40% say they don't know what their purpose is or remain neutral on the subject.

A study published in *Applied Psychology* found that people who had a sense of purpose, a feeling that their lives were meaningful, and a sense of control, live longer. Another study found that people with the strongest sense of well-being were more likely to live longer. Research also suggests a connection between positive health outcomes and a sense of purpose, including fewer heart attacks and strokes, a lower risk of disabilities and dementia, and better sleep. Additionally, a study published in the *Journal of Research and Personality* found that people who feel a sense of purpose have a higher income than those who don't find any meaning in the work they do.

With so many benefits, it only makes sense that you pursue your purpose—but most people don't know how. To find it, you'll need to do a lot of self-reflection, get feedback from others, and discover your passion. The good news is that self-reflection comes naturally to highly sensitive people, so you should find it a lot easier than most to find your purpose. Here are some tips to get you started:

- **Donate Your Time, Talent or Money:** The most important habit to develop when it comes to finding your purpose is helping others. Research conducted by Florida State University found that meaningfulness and happiness were similar, but there was a fundamental difference between the two. Their study found that happiness was connected to receiving before giving. On the other hand, meaningfulness was linked to being a giver before a receiver. People who gave more in a relationship had a more purposeful life.

Altruistic behavior includes extending a helping hand on a day-to-day basis, donating money to a cause you are passionate about, or volunteering for a non-profit organization. Whether you volunteer to get your elderly neighbor's groceries once a week, or spend every other Sunday serving food at the soup kitchen, expressing kindness will give meaning to your life.

- **Listen to What Others Say About You:** Sometimes the things you are passionate about come naturally to you. And because it's something you do automatically, you don't see it as a passion. I've always been a gifted writer. From as young as I can remember, people have always come to me when they needed something written, and they would gush about how inspirational it was. I didn't see it as a gift until it was highlighted to me. One day, my manager pulled me to the side and asked if I'd ever considered writing a book because my writing ability was rare. He pointed out that there were not many people who could put words together the way I could. It was at that moment that I started thinking about it.

    Maybe your friends and family members think you're a great speaker and always ask you to give the opening speech at social gatherings, or your loved ones are always saying you can dance or make good flower arrangements. Whatever it is, pay attention to the compliments you get from the people around you to give you insight into what your passion might be. You can also ask friends, family members, and co-workers.

- **Your Inner Circle:** You read about the people you choose to have in your life in Chapter 6. But what I didn't mention is that these people will determine whether you find your purpose or not. Individuals who are living a purpose-driven life will inspire those around them to live a purpose-driven life. Meanwhile, negative energy drainers who are always complaining about how difficult life is have chosen misery over purpose. People who are fulfilling their purpose don't have time for negativity.

- **Start Speaking to People:** It's easy to bury your head in a book or your phone when you're waiting at a bus stop or the subway. Instead, use this time to speak to the people around you. Ask what they like doing in their spare time, or if they're working on any projects they're passionate about. Speak to them about whether they've found the true meaning of life—if so, ask how they found it; if not, as why not. Starting conversations with random people can be difficult for the highly sensitive because we are prone to social anxiety. However, you'll be amazed at the inspiration you can acquire from the random man sitting at the bus stop.

- **Develop Your Interests:** Is there a topic you are always talking about with friends and loved ones? Are you always sharing articles about human rights injustices or domestic violence? Do your friends on social media expect you to post pictures of you participating in certain activities such as cooking or gardening? The conversations you enjoy and the things you share on social media will give you insight into your life's purpose.

- **Think About Injustices That Anger You:** Some people are passionate about the many injustices that take place around the world. Is there anything that deeply saddens you? Is there anything that makes you angry when you think about it? It might be a civil rights issue, animal welfare, or old people spending the holidays alone. Whatever the issue, there are a lot of organizations out there who could do with your help. You don't need to give up your job to engage in your purpose; your career might provide the financial stability you need to donate to causes and participate in the things you're passionate about.

- **Think About What You Love Doing:** Do you love watching ballerinas or ice skaters dance? Do you love taking part in extreme sports? Your skills might be best put to use bringing these things to children who also love them but don't get to do them. Or maybe you love working with numbers—how about volunteering to help teenagers improve their math skills?

Whatever passions, talents, and skills you can bring to the table, start looking for ways to turn your passions into something that will bring meaning into your life. Finding your purpose isn't going to happen overnight. I can't tell you how long it's going to take, but you can only do it one step at a time. Bear in mind that finding your purpose doesn't mean you have to walk away from your current job. Sometimes, it's about finding purpose in what you're already doing. If you're a hairdresser or a makeup artist, your purpose could be in the joy you get from making others feel beautiful. If you wash cars for a living, you can find purpose in making people feel happy about having a shiny-looking car. If you're a schoolteacher, you might find purpose in providing the right environment for your students to thrive. Remember, everyone has a purpose. It's up to you to find yours.

Become the Best Version of Yourself: What does becoming the best version of yourself actually mean? I heard this a lot growing up, but it was never explained, and so you make assumptions about it. Does it mean becoming super fit and healthy? Or attaining the highest level of education such as a doctorate degree? The answers I found fell short of my expectations, and when I started my journey of self-discovery as a highly sensitive person, I started asking myself important questions that led me to understand how I could optimize personal growth and become the best version of myself.

Becoming the best version of yourself means becoming who you were originally supposed to be. I know that sounds strange, but hear me out. We were put on the earth to grow into supreme, powerful beings who conquer the world. Unfortunately, the majority of us were not raised in the right environment, and it hindered our personal growth. Although I love my parents and they gave me the only tools for optimal living they knew how to give, they didn't teach me how to thrive. I've become who I am not because of the principles and values I was raised with, but because I got to such a low place in life that I was forced to search for meaning. Now that I know what it takes to become the best version of yourself, I want to share it with you:

- **Stop Limiting Yourself:** You know yourself because you see yourself every morning when you look in the mirror. You know what stage of life you're at, and whether you're happy about it or not. But what you don't know is who you could become. And this is because our limiting beliefs hold us back. When you let go of your limiting beliefs, you will start moving towards the life you know you deserve.

- **Focus on Your Strengths:** It's human nature to focus on your weaknesses, but instead of trying to improve them, we use them as an excuse not to strive for our goals. In doing so, we neglect our strengths—and it is our strengths that will help us reach our goals. Stop thinking about what you're not good at and keep practicing what you are good at. When you start excelling in that area, you'll find a confidence that you never knew you had, and that will push you in the direction you need to go in to reach your full potential.

- **Shed Your Old Identity:** If you're going to become the best version of yourself, you've got to let go of some things—and that means the person you are now. This is perhaps one of the most difficult things to do because you are surrounded by people who expect you to act and speak in a certain way. When you start changing your behaviors and speech, they can no longer identify with you and will do everything in their power to remain connected to your former self. But you've got to drop your bad habits and the way you think about yourself. Start living from the place you want to be and not from where you are now.

- **Silence Your Fears:** It is often said that "fear" stands for FALSE EVIDENCE APPEARING REAL. In other words, fear is an illusion. You are only fearful because of what you think is going to happen and not because of what you know is going to happen. Now, it would be unrealistic to tell you to ignore your fears; it's a natural human emotion and even the boldest people experience it. But what I *am* telling you to do is to do it scared. It took me years to release my first book because I was afraid it wouldn't be good enough. That fear didn't leave me, and it still hasn't. I released the book afraid, and what I learned is that, as Jack Canfield says, everything you want is on the other side of fear. You'll never know what you're capable of until you push through your fears.

Be a Giver: Highly sensitive people are givers by nature, but I believe that giving is human nature. The problem is that we live in a world where selfishness is applauded; everything is about self—"What can I acquire? How much money can I make? How can I get my needs met?" But research suggests that people who give their time and resources are happier. A survey conducted by the National Opinion Research Center found that people who gave two to three times per year were happier than those who didn't. Hoarding what you have is an indirect way of saying that there's not enough to go around—yet we live in a universe with infinite resources. A scarcity mentality causes fear, and living in fear leads to anxiety and depression. You will hear people say that they'll start giving when they reach a certain point in life—but you've *always* got something to give.

One of my favorite motivational speakers, Tony Robbins, told a story about something that happened to him before he became successful. He only had $20 to his name, and his friend owed him some money, but he wasn't paying. Tony contacted him several times to ask when he could pay it back, but it seemed as if his friend was avoiding him. With his last $20, he decided he was going to buy some food. He made his way to a local diner, sat down and ate. As he was paying for his meal, he noticed a young boy walk in with a woman. The boy went up to a table and pulled a chair out for the lady to sit down. Tony was fascinated as he watched this interaction; he wanted to know what motivated a young boy to be such a gentleman. He walked up to the table and introduced himself to the young boy, and jokingly asked if he was taking the lady out on a date. The boy replied no, she was his mother, and she had raised him to treat women in this way. Tony was so amazed by this little boy's attitude that he took all the change left over from his $20 out of his pocket and gave it to the boy, telling him to pay for his mother's meal.

Tony left the restaurant with empty pockets and a full heart. Three days later, he opened his mail and there was a check from his friend for the money he was owed. He had also sent a couple of hundred dollars extra for the inconvenience. That was the last day Tony ever struggled with lack because he realized that *giving* was the key that unlocked the door to abundance.

Giving doesn't have to be about money, but you've been blessed with many gifts that you can offer the world. You can volunteer your time, you can give kindness, you can help someone learn something you're good at. Think about how you can become a giver and start giving. It will bring you a sense of joy and fulfilment that money can't buy.

The Things That Make Life Better For HSPs

Before you read this list, I would like to stress that some of these suggestions might not apply to you. The highly sensitive are not one monolithic group of people who all think and act the same. We are all unique in our own right, and some of the ideas mentioned on this list don't work for me, but they work for my highly sensitive friends. You know yourself more than anyone else knows you. Go through the list and see what appeals to you, then adapt and modify the recommendations according to your needs.

A Solid Routine: I've started with this because I believe it's an essential part of our survival strategy. Without a routine, I don't think I would have made it this far—the reason being that it takes discipline to do the things we need to do as HSPs to live a fulfilling life. Just like an athlete must practice daily to perfect their skills, so must an HSP practice the tips mentioned throughout this book to live a fulfilling life. There are probably better basketball players in the world than Magic Johnson, but because they didn't have the discipline to practice every day, they never made it to the NBA. It takes doing the extra that nobody else is willing to do to succeed at anything, and that includes being an HSP. Routine is important because the more you do something, the easier it becomes. Once it becomes a habit, it becomes a lifestyle. Think about it like brushing your teeth. The majority of people brush their teeth as soon as they wake up in the morning. That's because they've been trained to do so since childhood, and now they do it on autopilot.

Today, my HSP routine is performed on autopilot. It took me a while to get to this point, but once I did, there was no looking back. I no longer experience weeks of depressive episodes where I can't leave my house. Life is a lot simpler now, and my routine has really helped me achieve that.

Wind-Down Time: My wind-down time starts when I get in the car after work. I put on soothing music as I drive home. I then take a cleansing saltwater shower to rid myself of all the negativity I've encountered throughout the day. I have my dinner, write, or read a book for a couple of hours and then get ready for bed. When I get into bed, I write in my gratitude journal, visualize, and fall asleep listening to 417hz music. I do this every day, including the weekends. The only thing that's different is that I don't drive home from work. But if I go to the store, for example, I will listen to soothing music or a motivational speech on the way there and back.

A Quiet, Calm Place to Retreat: If you live with family, or you've got roommates, it's important that you have a quiet and calm place to retreat to, or you'll get overwhelmed. In Chapter 2, I provided some suggestions on how you can turn your bedroom into somewhere you can find peace.

Permission to Get Emotional: I've been accused of being overemotional, too sensitive, over the top—you name it, I've been called it. That's because the majority of people don't understand high sensitivity, and I don't judge them for that. The reality is that you are only going to get permission to be emotional from the people who understand you. To anyone else, you are going to become an irritant. It goes back to making sure you've got the right people in your life, so you are not made to feel uncomfortable being who you are.

A Healthy, Gentle Way to Manage Conflict: Highly sensitive people don't like conflict. We would rather avoid it than get into an argument with someone. But avoiding conflict is just as unhealthy as dealing with conflict in a way that doesn't serve either party. In life, we are going to have conflicts with friends, family members, co-workers, and romantic partners. Having conflict isn't the problem, the way we resolve it is. Unfortunately, there will be times when you'll just need to cut your losses and move on because some people are just unreasonable, and no matter how much you try and come to a resolution, they will refuse to compromise. In such instances, I would advise that you agree to disagree and go your separate ways.

Non-Alcoholic and Caffeine-Free Options: As you've read in Chapter 3, caffeine can cause anxiety, and alcohol disrupts your sleep. Highly sensitive people don't need either. If you want to feel as if you're having a glass of wine, drink a non-alcoholic option; and drink decaf coffee, it tastes the same, but it's free from caffeine.

People Who Respect Your High Sensitivity: The worst thing for a highly sensitive person is to be surrounded by people who don't respect their sensitivity. As stated, I have gone no-contact with several immediate family members because of this, and I don't regret it one bit. They would regularly mock me and make sarcastic comments about it. They were loud and boisterous when I was around them, knowing full well that I can't take noise. I hated going to family gatherings because I would end up terribly depressed for a good couple of weeks afterwards. But I felt obliged to attend because I was family. I believe family is important, but your own personal happiness is way more important. Anyone who disturbs your peace should be eliminated from your life.

It sounds extreme, but think about it like this: if your friend was in an emotionally abusive relationship that destroyed her sense of self-worth, and her partner triggered depressive episodes every time they saw each other, would you advise her to stay in the relationship? Any sane person is going to tell her to run and not look back. So why do we tolerate the same type of abuse from family members?

An Outlet for Your Creativity: Every highly sensitive person I have ever met has been extremely creative. It's important to have an outlet for releasing your creativity or you'll get frustrated. I love to write—I'm an author—but outside of that, I'll journal and write about how I'm feeling in a very intense way. I always feel a lot better afterwards.

A Healthy Meal Schedule: I don't know about you, but when I get hungry, I get really irritated and I can't concentrate. Highly sensitive people feel everything more than the average person, and that includes hunger. I prevent hunger by eating small meals every four hours. I always carry a packet of nuts, whole-wheat crackers, fruit, or any other sugar-free snacks just in case I get hungry in between my meals.

In the final chapter, you will learn about the importance of self-care, and some tips on nurturing your physical, emotional, and spiritual needs.

CHAPTER 10:

SELF-CARE TIPS FOR HIGHLY SENSITIVE PEOPLE

Let's get one thing straight: self-care isn't about being selfish or self-indulgent. Self-care means looking after your physical, mental, and emotional well-being so you can be effective in every area of life. According to Google Trends, searches for "self-care" have more than doubled since 2015. Dr. Paula Gill Lopez from the University of Fairfield Connecticut says there is a definite need for self-care because we have an epidemic of depression and anxiety. Wellness expert Kelsey Patel explains that self-care is the answer to the stress we are constantly exposed to. Today, it's stressful just keeping up with the pace of life. Technology continues to advance so dramatically that if you don't keep up, maintaining contact with your loved ones becomes difficult. As a result, people struggle to slow down and unwind, which makes them feel more overwhelmed and anxious.

WHY SELF-CARE IS SO IMPORTANT

According to The World Health Organization, self-care is "how individuals, families, and communities maintain their health and prevent illness." This definition focuses on physical health, and includes medical care and nutrition. It involves all the strategies people can implement to maintain their health and well-being. Other groups such as the Cover Clinic refer to self-care as the ability to implement coping strategies to deal with the stressors of life. According to licensed psychologist Dr. Marni Amsellem, the term "self-care" has broadened as it's become more mainstream and now focuses on anything you do to meet your own needs. This can include relaxing and calming activities or physical, spiritual, or intellectual practices.

Self-care is about having a meeting with yourself to see how you're feeling and what your body needs in order to feel better. Self-care means different things to different people, and as a highly sensitive person, you are going to have very specific needs that only you are aware of. Your idea of self-care can also change depending on your circumstances. Regardless of how you define self-care, engaging in it on a regular basis can help you maintain the best version of yourself. Research suggests that when self-care is practiced consistently, it reduces stress, boosts the immune system, boosts confidence, and increases productivity.

Types of Self-care

There are three broad categories of self-care:

- Physical self-care
- Emotional self-care
- Spiritual self-care

Physical Self-care

Physical self-care involves taking care of your body. Here are some physical health care tips:

Get Plenty of Sleep: For the average person, sleep is a necessity, but for highly sensitive people, it can make or break your day. Sleep does a lot of things, and one of them is that it calms and resets our overworked nervous system. I've mentioned this first because sleep is one of the most important self-care practices highly sensitive people can implement. Everyone is different, but I need eight hours of sleep a night—even an hour less will shut me down for the day. Unfortunately, despite the fact that HSPs need more sleep than others, we also find it more difficult to get to sleep because of our overworked nervous systems. This is where a strict nighttime routine comes in handy.

Eat Well: I discussed diet in Chapter 3; however, what I didn't mention is that you should eat according to how your body reacts to food. Even some of the healthiest foods can make you feel bad. For example, high-sugar fruits make me anxious, so I don't eat them. Mangos, cherries, grapes, and pears are the main culprits. Don't just eat foods because experts say they're good for you. Some of my highly sensitive friends are vegan because they feel sick when they eat animal products. What they're really feeling is the pain the animals go through when they are killed. Again, nutritionists say that fish is good for you, but for some highly sensitive people, it's not the case.

Take Pride in Your Surroundings: Your living environment is critical to your mental health. Mess, clutter, and chaos is a no-no for highly sensitive people. Whatever your living arrangement, keep it orderly or you'll find it difficult to function.

Look Good: Michelle Obama said it best: "When you look good, you feel good." And I've found this to be true. It doesn't matter if I'm spending the day alone—I always do my hair and makeup. Unfortunately, despite how much better it makes us feel, the assumption is that we want to look good because we're either vain or insecure. I've learned to ignore such comments and just do *me*. Additionally, I get my fingernails and toenails manicured once a week. A lovely lady comes to my house and does them for me. It's a really relaxing experience.

EMOTIONAL SELF-CARE

By prioritizing your emotional self-care, you'll feel a lot more fulfilled and happy with your life. Emotional self-care involves identifying and nurturing your conscious inner state and feelings. I found it easier to take care of my physical needs than my emotional needs because they're more visible. Here are some emotional self-care tips that work for me:

Pay Attention to Your Inner Voice: Negative thinking is something we all experience. That nagging inner voice that never seems to shut up… I call mine "Nigel." Negative thinking affects highly sensitive people more because we process our thoughts on a deeper level. As a result, we can get lost in those thoughts, and sometimes they become our reality. One of the strategies I use when I catch myself entertaining negative thinking is to turn it into a positive affirmation. For example, "You'll never be able to speak in front of all those people" becomes, "I am a powerful speaker who has something to say that people want to hear."

Create Boundaries: I discussed boundaries in Chapter 6; they are an important emotional self-care tip because they protect you from other people's energy. You can't let everyone into your space—they will drain and overwhelm you and leave you in a state of depression. Make sure you enforce boundaries at all times.

A Healthy Support System: You need people around you who understand what it means to be a highly sensitive person. You need a healthy support network that you can confide in when the going gets rough. To the average person, crying because you accidently saw someone get shot in a movie doesn't make sense. As you've probably experienced, what people don't understand, they judge, and for the sake of your mental health, you don't need judgment—you need unconditional love.

Identify Your Emotional Triggers: What are the things that trigger your negative thoughts and emotions? One of my main triggers was social media. If I wasn't in the right space in terms of where I was going in life, looking at accomplished friends and family on social media was really depressing. One of my self-care tips was to disable all my social media accounts until I had accomplished at least one goal. I do use social media today, but don't spend a lot of time on it.

Daily Meditation: Meditation is good for the mind; it helps you get in touch with and communicate with your soul on a deeper level. It helps you know yourself better and strengthens your emotional resilience.

Self-Compassion: Be kind to yourself. It's easy to be overly critical and focus on the things you don't like about yourself. I find it really helpful to write myself a love letter once a week. I tell myself how great I am, how proud of myself I am for everything I've accomplished during the week, and anything else that lets me know how spectacular I am!

Spiritual Self-Care

Highly sensitive people will understand this better than anyone else because we sense the spiritual world in a way that others don't. There are three elements to human beings: body, mind, and spirit. When it comes to self-care, the spirit is often overlooked in favor of physical and emotional self-care. Spiritual self-care means nourishing the soul by tuning into your higher self so you know what it needs. Here are some tips on maintaining your spiritual health:

Yoga: Most people associate yoga with physical self-care because it involves moving the body. Yes, yoga does have many physical benefits, but it's also very spiritual, and you will often hear yogis make reference to the seven spiritual laws of yoga:

- **Dharma:** The word "Dharma" refers to purpose. It is believed there is a purpose for everything in life. Yogis believe that true fulfilment and joy is discovered by using your gifts and talents to make the world a better place.

- **Detachment:** Since everything will turn out the way it's supposed to in the end, allowing the stresses of life to upset you is pointless.

- **Intention and Desire:** When your pure intentions are clearly defined and you submit them to the infinite potential of the universe, it becomes a lot easier for the desires of your heart to become your reality.

- **Least Effort:** Life will be a struggle if you fight with the universe. However, accepting how life unfolds and advancing in the direction it takes you will lead you to your true purpose.

- **Karma:** Aim for kindness in all your actions, because the energy you give to the universe will come back to you.

- **Giving and Receiving:** If you want to keep the positive flow of energy in the world, everything you give and accept should be positive.

- **Pure Potential:** Everything in the universe is connected, and that includes you. Therefore, if the universe's potential is limitless, so is yours.

Spend Time With Nature: Highly sensitive people have a special connection with nature; we are mesmerized by the awesomeness of living things. One of the reasons we love nature so much is that we crave environments that are calm and quiet, as well as stunning to look at. Forest bathing is one of my favorite things to do. It's a Japanese practice referred to as *Shinrin-yoku*, which translates to "taking in the atmosphere of the forest," or "forest bathing." It involves spending time in the forest amongst the trees. The Western world has been taking it seriously for a while, and it is used in therapeutic practices. Several studies have found that forest bathing has a number of health benefits:

- Reduces anxiety, depression, and confusion
- Increases vitality and energy, and reduces fatigue
- Relaxes the body and reduces stress by lowering cortisol levels

- Lowers blood pressure
- Boosts the production of NK cells, which fight bacterial infections and cancer
- Boosts the immune system and improves overall well-being
- Elevates mood
- Increases creativity and intuition

To forest-bathe, simply go into the forest and immerse yourself in the natural world. Get in touch with your senses, paying attention to touch, smell, taste, hearing, and sight. Walk around mindfully and slowly, taking deep breaths as you take note of your environment. Can you feel the warm sunlight on your body? Can you hear the leaves crunching as you walk? How about the soft texture of pine needles? Can you smell the trees? What color are the leaves?

Sit in Silence: We live in a crowded, noisy, and overstimulated world that hates silence. You can't go anywhere without hearing noise; people can't walk down the street without talking on the phone, and every store has music playing. You can't get a lift from a friend without listening to the radio. Noise pollution is a very real problem, and not just for highly sensitive people. The Environmental Protection Agency states that it can cause sleep disturbance and high blood pressure. Indeed, there are many health benefits associated with silence. Here are some of them:

- Reduces blood pressure
- Improves the immune system
- Promotes new cell growth in the brain: a study conducted in 2013 discovered that new brain cells were formed

in the hippocampus as a result of sitting in silence for two hours. This area of the brain is linked to emotions, remembering, and learning.
- Reduces stress by lowering adrenaline and blood cortisol levels. A 2006 study found that two minutes of silence helped alleviate tension in the brain and body. This was caused by changes in blood circulation in the brain, and blood pressure.
- Prevents a build-up of plaque in the arteries

Expand Your Knowledge: Education shouldn't stop after high school or college. Experts state that reading is to the mind what exercise is to the body: it strengthens it. If you want to reach your highest potential, continuous learning is a must. When you are competent, it increases your confidence in your capabilities. Learning new concepts and ideas expands the mind and opens the door to new opportunities.

Focusing on self-care is definitely one of the best things I've ever done for myself, and I'm sure you will have the same experience. When you take the time out to look after yourself, you will have more to give others—and that's what we strive for as highly sensitive people.

CONCLUSION

Now, highly sensitive brothers and sisters, it's time to get to work! I know how easy it is to get comfortable chilling in your discomfort. But what you don't want is to hit rock bottom before you decide to take action—because unfortunately sometimes that's what it takes. I knew there was something wrong with me for years, but I did what I do best and buried my feelings. It wasn't until I started therapy that I learned one of the main reasons for not wanting to confront my dysfunction was because I knew it would take work to get out of it. I had also arrived at a destination called "acceptance," and I didn't mind remaining there. I could never have envisioned that the simple act of putting one foot in front of the other and walking myself out of my cocoon would lead me to where I am today. And that's what I want you to do: start taking baby steps.

You're not going to get it overnight—healing is a journey and it takes a while to get there. Some days are going to be better than others, but I can promise you that you will get there if you are determined to keep trying. Living in a state of anxiety, constantly feeling overwhelmed and battling against the evils of negative energy is no walk in the park. It feels like you're carrying dead weight, and a lot of highly sensitive people have found ways to accommodate that weight. We live with that feeling of dread in the pit of our stomach, fear becomes the norm, and we often feel as if we are drowning in a sea of despair. But you don't have to live like this.

Unfortunately, there's no easy way out. Like every good thing in life, it's going to take hard work on your part. I wouldn't be where I am today if I hadn't applied the strategies I was given. Reaching your highest potential is like climbing to the top of a mountain without any protective gear. You are going to get bruised and bloody, and sometimes you'll start making headway, and then fall all the way back to the bottom. But you've got to keep going because, as the saying goes, "Everything you've ever wanted is on the other side of fear."

You might feel a little overwhelmed by the information in this book. It's the accumulation of years of research with all the best bits compiled in short form. The first step I took on my highly sensitive journey was to get my house in order. My therapist told me to start there, and to date, it's the best piece of advice I've ever been given. I want to give you the same advice—once your home becomes a sanctuary, everything else falls into place. You will find that you sleep better, and you're not waking up disheveled and disorientated first thing in the morning. The second step is to write out a daily routine. I started with meditation, and once this became a habit, I started adding more to it. The third step is to write a list of everything you need to do the following day. Once you've got these three strategies down to a science, you'll start operating in flow mode, and you'll start blooming in your gift.

Finally, I implore you not to give up. The world needs you, people need you, and the gift you possess will make a powerful impact if you just keep running with it.

I wish you blessings, peace and prosperity as you embark on your journey to become the most powerful version of yourself as a highly sensitive person!

THANKS FOR READING!

I really hope you enjoyed this book and, most of all, got more value from it than you had to give.

It would mean a lot to me if you left an Amazon review—I will reply to all questions asked!

Simply find this book on Amazon, scroll to the reviews section, and click "Write a customer review".

Or alternatively, please visit www.pristinepublish.com/hsp2review to leave a review

Be sure to check out my email list, where I am constantly adding tons of value. The best way to get on the list currently is by visiting www.pristinepublish.com/empathbonus and entering your email.

Here I'll provide actionable information that aims to improve your enjoyment of life. I'll update you on my latest books, and I'll even send free e-books that I think you'll find useful.

Kindest regards,

Judy Dyer

Also by
Judy Dyer

Grasp a better understanding of your gift and how you can embrace every part of it so that your life is enriched day by day.

Visit: www.pristinepublish.com/judy

REFERENCES

Acn, H. F. P. L. A. (2017). *Unfuck Your Brain: Getting Over Anxiety, Depression, Anger, Freak-Outs, and Triggers with science (5-Minute Therapy)* (Illustrated ed.). Microcosm Publishing.

Allen, S. (2018). *The Science of Generosity*.

Aron, E. N. (1997). *The Highly Sensitive Person: How to Thrive When the World Overwhelms You* (Reprint ed.). Broadway Books.

Aron, E. N. (2010). *Psychotherapy and the Highly Sensitive Person: Improving Outcomes for That Minority of People Who Are the Majority of Clients* (1st ed.). Routledge

Ayala, E.E., Winseman, J.S., Johnsen, R.D. and Mason, H.R.C. (2018). U.S. medical students who engage in self-care report less stress and higher quality of life. *BMC Medical Education*, 18(1).

Baker, M. (2007). *Music moves brain to pay attention, Stanford study finds*. News Center.

Baumeister, R.F., Vohs, K.D., Aaker, J.L. and Garbinsky, E.N. (2013). Some key differences between a happy life and a meaningful life. *The Journal of Positive Psychology*, 8(6), pp.505–516.

Bernardi, L., Porta, C. and Sleight, P. (2005). Cardiovascular, cerebrovascular, and respiratory changes induced by different types of music in musicians and non-musicians: the importance of silence. *Heart*, 92(4), pp.445–452.

Blanton, B., & Ferguson, M. (2005). *Radical Honesty: How to Transform Your Life by Telling the Truth* (Revised ed.). Sparrowhawk Publications.

Cascio, C.N., O'Donnell, M.B., Tinney, F.J., Lieberman, M.D., Taylor, S.E., Strecher, V.J. and Falk, E.B. (2015). Self-affirmation activates brain systems associated with self-related processing and reward and is reinforced by future orientation. *Social Cognitive and Affective Neuroscience*, 11(4), pp.621–629.

Childre, D. L., Martin, H., & Beech, D. (2000). *The HeartMath Solution: The Institute of HeartMath's Revolutionary Program for Engaging the Power of the Heart's Intelligence* (Reprint ed.). HarperOne.

Colbin, A. (1986). *Food and Healing: How What You Eat Determines Your Health, Your Well-Being, and the Quality of Your Life* (Reissue ed.). Ballantine Books.

Cornwell, E.Y. and Waite, L.J. (2009). Social Disconnectedness, Perceived Isolation, and Health among Older Adults. *Journal of Health and Social Behavior*, [online] 50(1), pp.31–48.

Dai, R. and Lim, L.-T. (2013). Release of Allyl Isothiocyanate from Mustard Seed Meal Powder. *Journal of Food Science*, 79(1), pp.E47–E53.

Digestive Health Team (2017). *3 Reasons You Crave Sweet or Salty Foods*. Health Essentials from Cleveland Clinic.

Eden, D., Feinstein, D., & Myss, C. (2008). *Energy Medicine: Balancing Your Body's Energies for Optimal Health, Joy, and Vitality* (Revised&enlarged ed.). Jeremy P. Tarcher.

Harvard Health. (2021). *Can meditation help your heart?*

Harvard Health Publishing (2019). *Use everyday habits to keep your memory in good shape - Harvard Health*. Harvard Health.

Harvard T.H. Chan School of Public Health (2019). *Energy Drinks*. The Nutrition Source.

Haynes, T. (2018). *Dopamine, Smartphones & You: A battle for your time*. Science in the News.

Hopkins Medicine (n.d.). *Fight Inflammation to Help Prevent Heart Disease*.

Kahneman, D. and Deaton, A. (2010). High Income Improves Evaluation of Life but Not Emotional Well-Being. *Proceedings of the National Academy of Sciences*, 107(38), pp.16489–16493.

Kirste, I., Nicola, Z., Kronenberg, G., Walker, T.L., Liu, R.C. and Kempermann, G. (2013). Is silence golden? Effects of auditory stimuli and their absence on adult hippocampal neurogenesis. *Brain Structure and Function*, 220(2), pp.1221–1228.

Kobau, R., Sniezek, J., Zack, M.M., Lucas, R.E. and Burns, A. (2010). Well-Being Assessment: An Evaluation of Well-Being Scales for Public Health and Population Estimates of

Well-Being among US Adults. *Applied Psychology: Health and Well-Being*, 2(3), pp.272–297.

Ma, A. S., & Lcsw, S. A. (2020). *The Highly Sensitive Person's Guide to Dealing with Toxic People: How to Reclaim Your Power from Narcissists and Other Manipulators*. New Harbinger Publications.

Morter, S., & PhD, T. J. B. (2020). *The Energy Codes: The 7-Step System to Awaken Your Spirit, Heal Your Body, and Live Your Best Life* (Illustrated ed.). Atria Books.

News North Western Education (n.d.). *Rhythm of breathing affects memory and fear*.

Novotney, A. (2019). The risks of social isolation. *American Psychological Association*.

Pacheco, D. (2020). *Alcohol and Sleep*. [online] Sleep Foundation.

Sand, I., & Svanholmer, E. (2016). *Highly Sensitive People in an Insensitive World*. Jessica Kingsley Publishers.

ScienceDaily. (n.d.). *Sensitive? Emotional? Empathetic? It could be in your genes*.

Stein, M.D. and Friedmann, P.D. (2005). Disturbed sleep and its relationship to alcohol use. *Substance abuse*, 26(1), pp.1–13.

Taking Charge of Your Health & Wellbeing. (2013). *What Is Life Purpose? | Taking Charge of Your Health & Wellbeing*.

UCLA. (n.d.). *UCLA Magazine*.